THE FAMILY STORY OF
BONNIE AND
CLYDE

THE FAMILY STORY OF
BONNIE AND CLYDE

PHILLIP W. STEELE
WITH MARIE BARROW SCOMA

PELICAN PUBLISHING COMPANY
Gretna 2000

First printing, February 2000
Second printing, June 2000

Library of Congress Cataloging-in-Publication Data

Steele, Phillip W.
   The family story of Bonnie and Clyde / by Phillip W. Steele
with Marie Barrow Scoma.
      p.   cm.
   Includes bibliographical references and index.
   ISBN 1-56554-756-X
   1. Parker, Bonnie, 1910-1934. 2. Barrow, Clyde, 1909-1934.
3. Criminals—United States—Biography. I. Scoma, Marie
Barrow, 1918-1999. II. Title.

HV6245 .S74 2000
364.15'52'092273—dc21
[B]

                                        99-054654

Printed in the United States of America

Published by Pelican Publishing Company, Inc.
1000 Burmaster Street, Gretna, Louisiana 70053

CONTENTS

FOREWORD

Those of you who have so kindly purchased this book—or at least picked it up off the shelf—must have commented to yourself, *Oh, no! Surely not another Bonnie and Clyde book.* In fact, I, too, made similar comments to myself when this project was first suggested to me. Over the past some seventy years, hundreds of books, articles, films, and video productions have, I thought, surely covered the story of Bonnie and Clyde. Why, then, would I even consider doing another version? It wouldn't have, in fact, been a consideration for me had I not received a telephone call one evening in 1998 from Charles Heard of Dallas, Texas.

Charles and I share a great many common interests, among which are recording our nation's old west and depression era history as accurately as possible for future generations. These common interests have been shared through our affiliations as members of the National Association for Outlaw and Lawmen history, commonly referred to as NOLA. Through NOLA, Charles became aware of my books on Jesse James, Belle Starr, the Civil War, and other subjects.

When Charles first met Marie Barrow Scoma, and learned of her desire to help prepare a text about her brother, Clyde

Barrow, and her family, he suggested that Marie and I get together. At age 81, Marie was most anxious to make her family's story known to the world before she died.

I first met Marie in January of 1998, and I learned why Charles was so right in telling me I would like her. This story is, therefore, the fulfillment of her desire to have the truth about her family recorded. According to Marie, no book, film, article, or video she ever read or saw told the Barrow Gang story completely or accurately. Although the final, unedited version of Marie's story was never reviewed by her before her untimely death, she had reviewed most of the first draft transcript while it was being prepared, and I believe it pleased her. I came to share her intense desire to see the Barrow story as Marie knew it preserved in print, and I am most grateful to Charles Heard for introducing me to her and recognizing the potential the two of us might reach by working together.

Before one can truly understand the stories of Bonnie and Clyde and other depression era gangs such as "Pretty Boy" Floyd, "Machine Gun" Kelley, John Dillinger, the Kimes Gang, Ma Barker, and others, it is necessary to understand the economic conditions the society faced during that period. Basking in the illusion of endless prosperity, the stock market boomed throughout the 1920s. In 1928, the unheard of level of 549 points continued to push our economy to new heights. In his inaugural address in March of 1929, President Herbert Hoover announced, "I have no fears about the future of this Nation. It is bright with hope."

Greatly enthused by such hope, thousands of schoolteachers, clerks, elderly retirees, and plant workers began to invest heavily in the stock market. As the summer months approached, however, a time of nervousness began to fall over our country. On October 24, later to be referred to as "Black Thursday," the stock market plunged. Within a week's time, over $15 billion dollars worth of stock investments had somehow disappeared, and there was no end for the plunge in sight. The economy was devastated, and it would not fully recover for twelve years.

The effects of the Great Depression were global, giving rise to political chaos throughout the world. The Hitler-led National Socialist (Nazi) Party was the strongest to emerge from the economic turmoil, leading to the World War II.

In 1930, America's society began to suffer the fallout of the depression. Four and one half million people lost their jobs that year. By the end of 1931, over eight million were jobless, and by 1932, the figure had risen to over fourteen million. The Hoover administration apparently had no answers. Some of the Hoover-led legislation even seemed absurd, such as approving a $45 million appropriation to help feed cattle affected by a 1930 drought, yet opposing a $25 million farm aid bill to help farm families. Our nation's noted comedian and beloved philosopher Will Rogers commented, "You can get a new road anywhere, but you can't get a sandwich in America."

As our country's social structure changed, our cities found unemployed and homeless citizens gathering on street corners. Wives assumed the role of breadwinner as banks forced foreclosures of farms and homes throughout the land. Those blessed with willing relatives were fortunate to be welcomed into their homes, while others gathered in tent cities that soon became known as "Hoovertowns" or "Hoovervilles."

Jobless American families were forced to survive in any way possible. Sending children into the woods to pick dandelions, wild mushrooms, and onions for "Hoover soup" was common. The Barrow family was faced with similar conditions, and they found common bonds with other farm families around the campfires and tents of west Dallas. Most, especially the tough Southern farmers, learned to cope with the economic hardships. There were others, however, who took a different course and allowed their solid childhood and social teachings to be whisked away by the harsh winds of economic crisis. Thieves and predators were created out of personal desperation. Such were the conditions in which Bonnie and Clyde became notorious.

PHILLIP W. STEELE

ACKNOWLEDGMENTS

Special thanks to the following for their help in researching, composing, and editing this text:

Jan Cooper, My Office Publishing, Fayetteville, Arkansas;

Connie Potter, Connie's Secretarial Service, Springdale, Arkansas; and,

Elaine Hopper and Jaleta Boyd, Springdale, Arkansas, secretaries to the author.

Along with special thanks to Charlotte Steele, wife of co-author Phillip W. Steele, for her research assistance and understanding of the many hours of quiet time necessarily taken by her husband during the preparation of this text.

This author cannot begin to be humble enough to recognize all of those who have volunteered their research time, encouragement, enthusiasm, purpose, and reasons for here constructing another text about Bonnie and Clyde. Those who need to be recognized the most for their help are as follows. Dozens of others also have contributed as well I know, and should I have overlooked such others, please forgive me.

Lillian Marie Barrow Scoma

Certainly leading the list of all who assisted in putting together what we hope to be the most accurate account ever presented about Bonnie and Clyde would be my co-author, Marie Barrow Scoma, Clyde Barrow's youngest sister. Had Marie not contacted me through a mutual friend in Dallas, it is most doubtful this author would have attempted such a book. Marie carefully explained to me at our first meeting in early 1999 that she felt the story of Bonnie and Clyde was yet to be told. Marie felt that all former presentations contained a great deal of off-the-wall fiction to create excitement. She wanted the true story, as she lived it with her brother Clyde and the Barrow family, to be told before her life ended.

After my first meeting with Marie, our day-long tour of Barrow family historic sights in Dallas, and having the opportunity to have the first glimpse by anyone outside the family of a daily diary kept by Clyde's mother, I realized there definitely was a story here that needed to be recorded. After getting to know the wonderful lady, I began to share her concerns. This resulted in an agreement between Marie, last of the Barrow family, and me to create a new book which will hopefully earn respect as the most accurate story every told about Bonnie and Clyde, their families, and their associates.

Over the succeeding weeks, I grew to greatly admire Marie and to share her intense desire to separate for the last time facts from folklore in the never-ending story of Bonnie and Clyde. Regrettably, as the final draft of this manuscript was nearing completion, Marie died quite suddenly from both heart and diabetes complications on February 2, 1999. She was age 81. Thankfully, Marie had been consulted on most all of the story presented here before her death; therefore, this story is her story and hopefully will please those who knew the story best.

Shawn Ray Scoma

Upon the sudden death of Marie Barrow, I found it necessary to call on Marie's only son Shawn to wrap up needed details and theories Marie had meant to cover. Shawn had heard his family stories and details being discussed throughout his lifetime and after his mother's death kindly came forth to assist in the book's completion. Shawn tragically lost both his mother and father Luke Scoma within thirty days, yet he realized the importance of publisher deadlines and respected his mother's wishes to see this book about his family completed rapidly.

Charles Heard

If acknowledgements should be placed in order of their importance, then Charles Heard, a Dallas stockbroker, collector, and avid historian, should head the list. All this began as a result of a phone call I received one evening from Charles. Through our common memberships in several old West historical societies, Charles had read my books on Jesse James, Belle Starr, and other subjects. He apparently liked the somewhat uncomplicated and accurate manner I used in preparing other non-fiction studies of American outlaw personalities. Charles had also come to know Marie Barrow and became familiar with the story she had to tell. He recommended that Marie and I at least meet and discuss the possibility of this co-authored project. Thanks, Charles, for everything you have done from the beginning to the end in bringing this text to reality. I know you miss Marie, as I do. I feel she would be proud.

Paula Marinoni

A Northwest Arkansas history preservation activist from Fayetteville, Arkansas, Paula has carefully researched activities of the Barrow gang for many years. W. D. Jones, Buck Barrow, and Buck's wife Blanche came through Fayetteville in 1933 and robbed Brown's Grocery Store while Bonnie and Clyde waited for them in a Fort Smith tourist cabin. Recognizing that this seemingly insignificant event was an important part of the region's depression era history, Paula has helped save the old store from the wrecking ball so far, and her support of this writer's efforts to record the true history of the Barrows in Northwest Arkansas is greatly appreciated.

Kenneth Butler

This old friend from Shawnee, Oklahoma, I first met over a cold beer in a Cheyenne, Wyoming, hotel lounge, and we have remained good friends ever since. I have always deeply admired Ken for his wealth of knowledge and historical detail about almost any personality we study from old West or American depression era history.

The Barrows spent a great deal of time in Oklahoma, and when Ken learned of this Barrow gang project, he wasted no time in sending me copies of the research he has done on the subject over the years. Not only has Ken saved me a great deal of time in preparing this book, but he has also helped preserve the accuracy we always strive to capture. Thanks, Ken, for all your help over the years.

Cleo Loyd

Another citizen of Northwest Arkansas, Cleo Loyd first contacted me many years ago about our common interest in regional history. Since that first meeting, I have grown to admire Cleo very highly for his research ability and dedication to separating facts from fiction when studying personalities like Bonnie and Clyde. I especially admire Cleo's willingness to openly share his research with me.

Through Cleo's interest in such research, we can be assured of accuracy in the facts presented in this text relating to the Fayetteville store robbery, the Barrow's Joplin gunfight, the Platte City affair, the shoot out at Dexter, Iowa, the Alma incident, and other events as reported through newspaper accounts.

Wanda Audit Brown Montgomery

While research for this project was underway, Wanda Audet of Camarillo, California, learned of it and openly offered to share her knowledge of the Barrow Gang's robbery of Brown's Grocery Store in Fayetteville. Living next door to the store and observing what actually took place at the store during the robbery, Wanda has added further firsthand source material so important in recording accurate history.

Thanks, Wanda, for volunteering the valuable information you had.

Ann Cooper

Another primary source interviewed by Cleo Loyd, his research assistant, and me was the daughter of R. L. Brown, owner of the site of the Brown's Grocery Store robbery. Ann, along with her brother George Brown of Hot Springs, Arkansas, provided invaluable firsthand information. Built in 1924, Brown's Store provided a living for the Brown family until the store was sold in 1948.

H. A. ("Tony") Perrin

As the Regional Supervisor for Region II, Arkansas Department of Parks and Tourism, Tony has researched, studied, and written about our Nation's depression era outlaws and lawmen for many years, especially about those who often took refuge in Arkansas. Tony's work is highly respected and, therefore, has been referred to in search of accuracy many times while preparing this text. Thanks, Tony, for all you have done and continue to do toward preserving accuracy in our state and nation's history.

Gene Harwood

Gene Harwood, a collector of historical data on the lives and times of Bonnie and Clyde for many years, was recommended as a possible source of accurate information.

Our first meeting resulted in several interviews and questions which have certainly helped separate facts from the volumes of fiction and folklore surrounding Bonnie and

Clyde. A citizen of Hot Springs, Arkansas, Gene was found to be overly generous in providing help and guidance to me.

Lorraine Joyner

Anyone who ever had the occasion to meet Lorraine Joyner of Gibsland, Louisiana, not only remembers this enthusiastic lady fondly, but also came away from that meeting with a better understanding of our Nation's depression era, and especially of the outlaw couple known as Bonnie and Clyde. Before Lorraine died in 1997, she had traveled the Nation giving lectures and sharing factual history about the lives and gruesome deaths of Bonnie and Clyde. Lorraine first encouraged me to proceed with this book, and I regret deeply that I did not get to meet Marie Barrow Scoma prior to Lorraine's death. I will, however, always cherish the time I spent with Lorraine and be forever thankful to her for her encouragement toward learning more about this intriguing subject.

Flo Stewart

A schoolmate of Bonnie Parker at Lanier High School in the West Dallas region known as Cement City, Flo Stewart spent a day with me in 1996, when she was age 89. Flo's enthusiasm for this project and the vivid memories she possessed added a great deal of information about the real Bonnie Parker, whom Flo considered to be her best friend.

Lt. Col. (Ret.) Weldon E. Dowis

While serving as Captain of E Company, 144th Infantry, of the Texas National Guard in Dallas, Weldon Dowis, helped arrange for the two Browning Automatic Rifles used by the Texas lawmen who brought down Bonnie and Clyde in Louisiana in 1934. At age 95, Col. Dowis remains quite active and alternates living between Dallas and Hot Springs, Arkansas. Co-author Phillip Steele had occasion to interview Col. Dowis at his Hot Springs home on April 28, 1999. He remembered the details of his participation with the law-men as if it were yesterday and greatly contributed to the preparation of this text.

Chuck Knox

Chuck Knox of Palmer, Texas, located through detailed research the home in which the Barrows lived near a cotton gin where Clyde Barrow was born.

PHILLIP W. STEELE

Migrant fieldhands such as the Barrow family followed crop harvests throughout mid-America. (Photo courtesy of University of Arkansas, Special Collections)

⚜1⚜

THE BARROW FAMILY

Henry B. Barrow was the son of Jim and Marie Jones Barrow of Pensacola, Florida. Henry, born in Alabama on January 10, 1874, lost his father at age eleven, and thereafter followed the harvest throughout the South with his family. Having no time to attend school regularly, Henry remained illiterate until his death in Dallas on June 19, 1957.

Henry met Cumie Walker from Nacogdoches, Texas, while following the cotton harvest, and they were married in Cumie's family farm home near Swift, Texas, on December 5, 1891. Although the family was very poor, and had a difficult time feeding and clothing their children, they had seven children between 1894 and 1918. Naturally, the Barrow

H.B. and Cumie Barrow, parents of Clyde Barrow. (Photo courtesy of Marie Barrow Scoma)

children, out of necessity, had to begin work supporting
their family at early ages. The Barrow family genealogy is as
follows:

Henry B. Barrow
Born: January 10, 1874, Alabama
Married: December 5, 1891
Died: June 19, 1957, Texas

Cumie T. Barrow
Born: November 21, 1874
Married: December 5, 1891
Died: August 14, 1942

Henry and Cumie Barrow's children:
Elvin Wilson Barrow
Born: June 20, 1894
Died: 1947

Artie Adell Barrow
Born: March 30, 1899
Died: March 3, 1981

Marvin Ivan ("Buck") Barrow
Born: March 14, 1903
Died: July 29, 1933

Nellie May Barrow
Born: May 12, 1905
Died: 1968

Clyde Chestnut Barrow
Born: March 24, 1909
Died: May 23, 1934

L. C. Barrow
Born: August 13, 1913
Died: September 9, 1979

Lillian Marie Barrow
Born: May 27, 1918, Kerens, Texas
Died: February 3, 1999
(One son: Shawn Ray Scoma, born on November 29, 1967)

Barrow family photo. Clyde (with hat) stands on the left, next to his father, H. B. Barrow. Marie Barrow, coauthor of this book, appears second from right on first row. (Photo courtesy of Marie Barrow Scoma)

Marie, the youngest child in the Barrow family, married Luke Scoma on August 7, 1963, in Rockwall, Texas. Regrettably, Marie died suddenly on February 3, 1999, in Mesquite, Texas, from complications from diabetes and heart problems. Marie's son Shawn has helped bring this story to a close.

Marie Barrow Scoma at a young age. (Photo courtesy of Marie Barrow Scoma)

Marie Barrow, youngest child of the Barrow family. (Photo courtesy of Marie Barrow Scoma)

Marie Barrow Scoma featuring Clyde Barrow memorabilia at a Fort Worth collector's show in early 1999. (Photo by Phillip Steele)

Shawn Scoma (left), only son of Marie Barrow and Luke Scoma, reviewing Barrow family photos with coauthor Phillip Steele. (Photo by Mrs. Phillip Steele)

Marie Barrow Scoma at her Mesquite, Texas, home a few weeks before her death. (Photo by Phillip Steele)

Henry and Cumie Barrow with their daughter Marie (right). (Photo courtesy of Marie Barrow Scoma)

2

CLYDE

Clyde Chestnut Barrow, the fifth child of Henry B. Barrow and Cumie T. Walker Barrow, was born March 24, 1909, near Teleco, Texas, some thirty miles southeast of Dallas. He was often left in the care of his sister, Nell, who was five years older. The Barrow children were unintentionally neglected by their overworked and tired parents, as were millions of other children at that time.

Marie Barrow Scoma recalled that the only good times they had as children were on the very few occasions they went to the movies in towns near their campgrounds. Clyde was thrilled by the adventures of cowboy outlaws on screen and would imagine himself to be Jesse James for weeks after seeing a movie featuring such outlaws.

The family, following crop harvests, moved frequently, making it difficult to keep any of their children in school very long. The Barrows often found it necessary to divide up their children and leave them with various relatives in Corsicana, Mabank, Kerens, and other locations throughout Texas while following the harvests. The Barrows finally moved, with their children, to a west Dallas campground. The campgrounds along the railroad tracks in west Dallas were full of gypsies, vagrants, hobos, gamblers, and homeless people of all kinds—and other undesirables.

Home near cotton gin in Palmer, Texas, believed to be where Clyde Barrow was born, March 24, 1909. (Photos courtesy of Chuck Knox)

The Barrows camped nightly in large tents that were attached to a Springfield wagon containing all of the family's possessions. Although the Barrow children had little time to attend school, their mother Cumie realized the importance of an education, and constantly encouraged her children to remain in school. As for teaching her children social graces, it was almost impossible given the negative influences of the campground society, to which the children were exposed on a daily basis. Cumie Barrow was the religious cornerstone in the family as well, and recognized that it was important for her children to learn and follow God's teachings. She demanded that her children attend church and Sunday school as often as possible.

Marvin Ivan ("Buck") Barrow, the third child of Henry and Cumie, was born at Jones Prairie, Texas, in Milam County. Described by his Mother as being one of the most likeable of her children—playful and obedient as a youth—Buck seemed to enjoy attending church services more than her other children. Buck was described by his sister, Nell, as a quiet, slow-talking young man, much like his father. Buck married Margaret Heneger a short time after the family moved to the west Dallas campground. Like thousands of other tenant farm families of the period, the Barrows simply could not support their large family with their meager incomes, so it was necessary for Buck to seek ways to help the family.

Clyde Barrow. (Photo courtesy of Marie Barrow Scoma)

Clyde attended school, whenever possible, around the Cement City section of west Dallas and even took some high school courses at Sidney Lanier High School. Clyde developed an interest in music and playing the guitar while attending Lanier. Perhaps his musical interest offered Clyde a means of escape from the drudgery and stress-filled society he lived in. Clyde spent many Saturday afternoons gazing at musical instruments—especially guitars, banjos, and saxophones—in Dallas music store windows. Of course, the family could not afford to buy such instruments or music lessons, which prevented the development of Clyde's natural music abilities. His ability was discovered when he first learned the basics of the saxophone while staying with his sister Nell, whose husband was a professional musician with a traveling orchestra.

Clyde Barrow with his sisters, Artie (left) and Nell (right). (Photo courtesy of Marie Barrow Scoma)

Marvin Ivan ("Buck") Barrow, Clyde Barrow's older brother. (Photo courtesy of Marie Barrow Scoma)

At age seventeen Clyde found it necessary to also leave school. He had no problem finding employment, and took jobs with Proctor and Gamble, The Brown Cracker and Candy Company, United Glass, NuGrape Company, and the A and K Top and Body Shop, and as a messenger with Western Union. As his many job changes seem to point out, Clyde had problems with the authority figures he encountered. Normally a most pleasant person, Clyde had an explosive temper that he sometimes had difficulty controlling.

Clyde had always loved automobiles, and managed to buy his first one for only $50.00. It was around this time that Clyde began dabbling in criminal activity. He was first arrested, along with his brother, Buck, for apparently taking several turkeys from a neighbor a few days before Christmas 1926, without bothering to pay for them. Buck was sentenced to a week in jail, but Clyde was released. Not long after this somewhat minor offense, Clyde pulled his first armed robbery by holding up a drug store in the Oak Cliff section of Dallas. Then he teamed up with his brother Buck, Frank Clause, and a couple of other west Dallas friends to rob the Buell Lumber Company. The group was discovered and arrested; however, they were only questioned, then released. Because they were being watched closely, and being accused of most of the crimes around the neighborhood, the group left the Dallas area to successfully rob other establishments in Waco and Sherman, Texas.

Marvin Ivan ("Buck") Barrow, Clyde Barrow's older brother. (Photo courtesy of Marie Barrow Scoma)

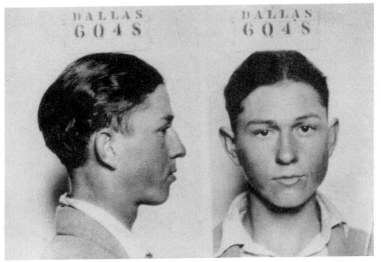

Clyde Barrow, Dallas jail mug shots. (Photo courtesy of Dallas Public Library)

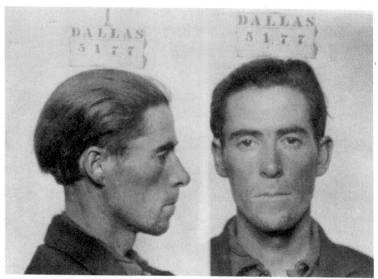

Marvin Ivan ("Buck") Barrow, Clyde Barrow's older brother. (Photo courtesy of Marie Barrow Scoma)

The Barrow "Star" station and garage in west Dallas. This building also served as the family home. (Photo courtesy of Marie Barrow Scoma)

❧3❧

THE OUTLAW GANG
IS FORMED

In October 1929, this group of rowdy young men, including Sidney Moore, managed to steal an automobile and race away to Denton, Texas, where they robbed a garage and took a safe—to be opened later. Clyde, the designated driver, attracted the attention of the local Denton police because he was driving fast, and for no apparent reason. Clyde soon wrecked the car, jumped out, and ran away, but Buck was shot trying to escape. Although it was generally known that Clyde Barrow participated in the theft, he was not implicated. Buck, however, was convicted and sentenced to a five-year term in the Texas State Penitentiary in Huntsville, Texas, on January 14, 1930. Sidney Moore, the other partner, received a ten-year sentence. This close encounter made Clyde realize that eventually he, too, would be caught and sent to prison if he continued to follow the "criminal" path.

Henry Barrow, with financial help from his daughter, Nell, managed to acquire a small frame home for his family near the campground. Soon afterward, Clyde helped his father convert the front part of the home into a gas station and garage, while they kept the back apartment for their living area. Recognizing Clyde's natural ability for repairing

The Barrow "Star" station and garage as it appears today. (Photo by coauthor Phillip W. Steele)

The Barrow "Star" station and garage in west Dallas (it also served as the family home). (Photo courtesy of Marie Barrow Scoma)

and servicing automobiles, Henry encouraged his son to help him develop a successful business. This offered Clyde his first opportunity to "own" his own business, and, at the same time, help his parents, brothers, and sisters establish roots and better survive the seemingly endless depression.

This surely must have been one of the happiest periods in Clyde's life—helping his father support the family and developing their own family enterprise must have given Clyde an inner peace and sense of self worth he had seldom, if ever, experienced in his deprived life. For the first time in years he was not being sought by the law, and his expertise at automobile repair was bringing in honest money. He was able to not only help support the Barrow family, but also find a bit of relaxation and fun for himself.

Clyde undoubtedly enjoyed bringing a little happiness into the lives of others sentenced by poverty to the west

Dallas campgrounds by playing his guitar around many a campfire. It was also during this period that Clyde took his natural music ability a bit further when he discovered the saxophone—the sax was an important instrument within the popular 1930s jazz music that was emerging. The fact that he must have loved his sax dearly becomes apparent when it is discovered that there was one with him, along with sheet music, when he was killed a few years later.

It didn't take long for Clyde to discover that his stylish new clothing and better grooming gave him confidence and opened some new doors. *I might even be handsome,* he may have thought. He began to notice girls, and, according to the diary kept by Mrs. Barrow, Clyde became involved with a group of wayward women in the neighborhood. Ignoring his mother's strong objections, Clyde knew a few young girls in the area who were willing to become prostitutes, so he began to promote their "assets" for a percentage of their fees.

Certain past Bonnie and Clyde biographers have indicated that Clyde Barrow may have had homosexual tendencies, since he often avoided female relationships. Certainly Clyde's short time promoting prostitution for his clients may have caused Clyde to lose some respect for women. According to Marie Scoma and other family members, however, Clyde was certainly not homosexual, and was, at least as far as they knew, normal in both matters of sex and affairs of the heart.

Marie Barrow, youngest of the Barrow children, with her brother, Clyde, at a family rendezvous near Dallas. (Photo courtesy of Marie Barrow Scoma)

Bonnie Parker (left) with her sister, Billy Jean Parker. (Photo courtesy of Marie Barrow Scoma)

Clyde Barrow (left) with his brother, L. C. Barrow. (Photo courtesy of Marie Barrow Scoma)

⊰4⊱

BONNIE PARKER EMERGES

Bonnie Parker was born a year later than Clyde on October 1, 1910, in Rowena, Texas, several miles southwest of Dallas. The Parkers were somewhat more comfortable than the average family at the time as a result of Henry Parker's master bricklaying skills.

Bonnie was described as being a somewhat mischievous, high-spirited child who was very well liked and admired by her peers. Actions in her adult life would indicate otherwise, but Bonnie was remembered as being a very tenderhearted young woman, who would cry easily. One example of Bonnie's kind spirit is vividly recalled by Flo Stewart from Longview, Texas. In 1996, at age 89, Flo explained how Bonnie always took time to assist her in walking or climbing stairs between classes at Cement City High School. A child-hood disease had left Flo seriously crippled, and she grew to sincerely admire Bonnie Parker for the kindness Bonnie showed towards her.

Bonnie was a very attractive young woman, which enchanted the boys, whom Bonnie loved to tease. At age fifteen, she met a handsome young man, Roy Thornton, who must have swept the fickle Bonnie off her feet with his youthful charm. By the time Bonnie had reached sixteen, she had married Thornton, thinking she had found her knight on his white horse to carry her away. Thornton, however, continually left his wife for months at a time, and Bonnie drowned her emotions in movies and romance magazines during the lonely days and nights. Roy finally left her in 1927, and did not return for two years. This time, obeying her mother's urgings, Bonnie refused to take Thornton back, even though he had been her first true love. Bonnie was only 19.

After this emotional upheaval, Bonnie went to west Dallas to visit a girlfriend who had fallen and broken her arm. Bonnie helped her friend with her housework, and Clyde Barrow, who also knew the girl, stopped by one day in January 1930 for a visit and to offer his assistance. This was the first meeting of Bonnie Parker and Clyde Barrow, a meeting from which a liaison would develop, the likes of which the country hasn't known since.

Apparently, it was love at first sight for both of them, and each seemed to find a meaningful and truly close relationship with each other.

Realizing how she felt about Clyde, Bonnie was thrilled to take him home to meet her mother. Friends have pointed out that Bonnie was extremely close and devoted to her mother, something that proved to be very difficult for her in later years.

Clyde spent the night on the couch at the Parker home. Since he was hoping to impress Bonnie's mother, he must have been terribly embarrassed when police came with arrest warrants for his participation in a Denton, Texas, robbery, as well as other robberies around Waco that Clyde had been in on with his brother Buck. A few weeks later, Bonnie wrote Clyde a letter in the Denton jail that fully outlined her true feelings.

"When you get out I want you to go to work, and for God's sake don't ever get into anymore trouble."

Still another letter pleaded:

"Honey, if you get out OK, please don't ever do anything to get locked up again."

Bonnie Parker in a sensual pose during one of the gang's breaks from driving. (Photo courtesy of Marie Barrow Scoma)

Bonnie Parker and Clyde Barrow at a family rendezvous near Dallas. (Photo courtesy of Dallas Public Library)

When Clyde was released from Denton, authorities from Waco, Texas and McClennan County asked that Clyde be transferred there for a hearing. Waco police went to Denton and escorted Clyde there on March 2, 1930.

By now, it had been quite some time since Bonnie had seen Clyde, and she begged her mother to loan her money for a bus trip to Waco so she could be with him. Mrs. Parker was horrified that her lovely daughter, who was still married to a criminal, had once again fallen in love with a social outcast. Bonnie was determined, though, to somehow find a way to Waco and finally convinced her mother she could stay there with her cousin, Mary, and would be perfectly safe. Cousin Mary's husband was a musician who traveled a great deal.

Mrs. Parker did not have funds for a bus ticket, so Bonnie rode to Waco with Clyde's mother on March 3, 1930, and moved in with Mary.

Clyde was placed in a jail block along with William Turner and three others. Turner was already a hardened criminal who had been convicted on several charges ranging from burglary to car theft. When Bonnie came to visit Clyde, Turner told her of a plan whereby he and Clyde could escape, with her help. Turner suggested that Bonnie visit his parent's home at 625 Turner Avenue in east Waco. His folks were expected to be out late that evening, and Bonnie could slip in, get Turner's gun, and bring it to Turner on her next jail visit. Bonnie immediately asked Clyde what he wanted her to do.

"It's a way to get me out of here and us together sooner," Clyde replied.

Turner explained to Bonnie that she should wait until dark.

"The front door will be locked, but a key can be found on the doorsill on the left side." He told her the gun could be found in a closet.

That evening, Bonnie convinced a very nervous Mary to drive her to the neighborhood. After considerable difficulty, they located the gun and raced out of the house. Afraid of being caught with a weapon, Bonnie and Mary went immediately to the jail, where Bonnie had no difficulty slipping the weapon to her lover. Bonnie had not only burglarized a home and taken a deadly weapon, but she had also smuggled into the jail a pistol that would later be used in the escape. These were the first known criminal activities of Bonnie's young life.

⚜5⚜

BARS WERE NOT
FOR THE BARROWS

Turner had devised a plan where, around 7:00 P.M., he would ask for a glass of milk to settle his "upset" stomach. According to jail procedure, the night jailer, I. P. Stanford, left his firearms in his office before taking the milk to Turner. Just as the jailer opened the cell door to hand the milk to Turner, Turner rushed the door and jammed Stanford's head and shoulder through the cell door just as another cellmate, Abernathy, brandished the pistol and spoke softly, "I'll kill you if you make a sound." Stanford recognized the desperation in the man's voice and simply raised his arms.

Clyde, Turner, and Abernathy ran out of the cellblock. As the escapees slipped down the stairs, "Turnkey" Jones was sitting at his desk on the jail's first floor, reading a newspaper. Abernathy pointed the gun toward Jones, while Clyde ran to one side of him and Turner to the other. Their literal "twisting" of his arms convinced the jailer to hand over the keys. Clyde rushed to the front door, unlocked it, removed the heavy oak bar, and ran outside to freedom, with Turner and Abernathy closely behind.

The trio noticed a green Ford, which belonged to Mrs. J. M. Byrd, parked along North 5th Street, a few blocks from the jail. They somehow hot-wired the engine, then climbed into the vehicle and raced away. Before leaving Waco, they stole another car as they drove west through Goldthwaite before turning north. Several other cars would be stolen along their route to help throw off pursuing authorities: one was stolen in Wichita Falls, Texas; one in Joplin, Missouri; and still another in St. Louis, Missouri. Continuing through Illinois, the trio indiscriminately robbed and burglarized homes and businesses along their route.

Bonnie left Waco and returned home to Dallas, where she nervously awaited a message from Clyde. Mrs. Parker tried her best to discourage Bonnie's feelings for Clyde, but she soon realized Bonnie was hopelessly in love. Bonnie seemed even closer to her lover as a result of her dramatic participation in his escape from the Waco jail. Clyde did finally send a Western Union message from Illinois to Bonnie pledging his love, promising to write, and asking Bonnie to notify his mother that he was okay.

Crossing into Indiana, the fugitives robbed still more businesses , and by March 18, 1930, had reached Middleton, Ohio. Newspapers there reported that one of Clyde's methods of operation was to steal automobile license plates and change them often to confuse pursuers. The practice proved to be successful in preventing his capture.

The group took $60.00 in the robbery of the Baltimore and Ohio Railroad ticket office. Breaking into a Middleton, Ohio, ladies store proved fruitless, as there was no cash, but they did manage to grab silk articles to send to their girlfriends.

Driving west from Middleton, the three escapees stopped for breakfast at an all-night diner. Around 8:00 A.M., two patrol cars drove through the west edge of the city just as Clyde and his associates pulled away from the diner and headed east. The lawmen began following them. Hoping to confuse their pursuers, Clyde slowed the car to let Turner and Abernathy escape on foot. Within a short time, the officers caught up with both Turner and Abernathy, who surrendered without resistance.

Clyde, unaware of the capture of his friends, returned and started cruising the neighborhood, hoping he could pick them up. Around 10:00 A.M. officers spotted Clyde and blocked his escape. Clyde drove over a curb, then between two houses, before smashing the car into an old canal. He then jumped from the car and ran, shooting occasionally at the pursuing officers with the revolver Bonnie had sneaked to him in the Waco jail. Fearing possible capture, Clyde threw the pistol into the canal.

Abernathy and Turner answered all the questions officers asked them. The men told them that the man who escaped was just a hitchhiker they had picked up along the road. This story was somewhat substantiated when officers captured Clyde and brought him in for questioning as well. Claiming to be Robert Thomas, from Indianapolis, Clyde refused to give the officers any further information.

Upon receiving the descriptions of the three men, Waco authorities County Sheriff Les Stegal and assistant District Attorney Jimmy Stanford boarded a train in Texas around 3:30 P.M. bound for Ohio, where they hoped to find Clyde, Abernathy, and Turner. Arriving at 12:30 A.M. the next day, March 21, the Texas officers picked up their prisoners and started back for Waco at once. The next day, back in Waco, the three handcuffed prisoners were transported from the train to the Waco jail without incident.

Clyde Barrow (left) with his mother, Cumie Barrow, at a family rendezvous near Dallas. (Photo courtesy of Dallas Public Library)

⊰6⊱

BACK TO PRISON

Clyde's troubles began to accelerate only a short time after his return from Ohio. He was accused of killing a man in Houston, Texas, nearly a year before his arrest. It turned out that the Harris County officials were simply looking for someone to blame for the murder there, and picked Clyde as being the most likely suspect soon after his Waco jailbreak. Authorities discredited depositions taken from alleged witnesses, and the case against Clyde was dropped.

Clyde's mother, along with Bonnie Parker, arrived in Waco on March 27, 1930, to visit their cherished Clyde before the state transferred him to the Texas Federal Prison in Huntsville. Hoping guards would go easy on him, Clyde told authorities he was only eighteen, and not his true age of twenty-one.

Clyde Barrow was transferred to Huntsville on April 21, 1930, and given the number 63527. It was at this time that he told authorities his middle name was "Champion" instead of Chestnut—for what reason, we do not know. Clyde also stated that Bonnie Parker was actually his wife so that he could continue to receive letters from her at the prison.

Further information recorded in the prison describes Clyde fully. Listed as being 5'7" in height and weighing 127

pounds, Clyde had brown eyes and dark hair. His distin-
guishing marks were listed as a tattoo—E. B. W.—on his left
forearm, another showing the letters U. S. N. on his inner
right forearm, and a third tattoo featuring a girl's head on
the outer part of his right arm. Shortly after his arrival at
Huntsville, Clyde was assigned to the Eastham Prison Farm,
forty miles north of the main prison in Huntsville, where he
began serving a fourteen-year term.

According to Cumie Barrow, her son was sodomized by a
large and over-powering inmate while at the Eastham facil-
ity. This traumatic treatment seriously affected young
Clyde, and he swore to kill the man if ever the chance arose.
While Clyde was still in prison, history records that Clyde's
abuser was murdered by an unknown party a short time
after he was released from prison. "The attack and sodomy
made Clyde mean as a snake," Clyde's sister later told the
family.

Bonnie was understandably devastated by her separation
from Clyde. Crying almost constantly, she was heartbroken
over the thought of not being able to have Clyde beside her
for such a long time. Because her letters to Clyde only
fueled her anguish and deep sadness, Bonnie finally
stopped writing, took a waitress job, and began going out
with almost anyone who asked her, just to help her get her
mind off of Clyde.

Throughout Clyde's first eight months in Waco, his
mother pleaded with District Judge R. I. Monroe to reduce
her son's sentence from fourteen years to two years.

Clyde's brother Buck decided to clear his name as well.
Buck had earlier simply walked away from a work detail at
Eastham Prison Farm, after which he met and married
Blanche Caldwell at McCurtain, Oklahoma, on July 3, 1930.
Blanche was the daughter of Mr. and Mrs. M. F. Caldwell of
Goodwater, Oklahoma. When Buck told his wife that he was
an escaped convict, Blanche and his mother joined togeth-
er to try and get Buck to turn himself in. Together they con-
vinced him, and two days after Christmas, in 1931, Buck's

Buck Barrow holding Blanche Barrow. (Photo courtesy of Marie Barrow Scoma)

family took him to Huntsville, where he surrendered to authorities.

Apparently unaware of his mother's efforts to get his sentence reduced, Clyde had become quite despondent. His small and weak stature made it difficult for him to keep up the workload assigned him at the prison farm. Clyde had heard rumors of Bonnie becoming tired of waiting for him and dating others, a fact that seemed to be confirmed because Bonnie's letters had become fewer and shorter.

Clyde's despondence tempted him to arrange for an injury, which might result in his getting better treatment—

he hoped. After convincing a fellow convict to help, Clyde faked an accident by having his inmate friend chop off two of his toes with an ax. Clyde's absurd plan actually worked; he was surprised, however, when he learned that his "injury" had not only gotten him out of a torturous work detail, it had actually speeded up his parole, as well. Soon Governor Ross Sterling answered Mrs. Barrow's faithfulness to her son by agreeing to parole Clyde. He was released from prison on February 8, 1932, still on crutches from the deliberate injury.

Back in Dallas, the family was noticeably disturbed over the obvious changes they noticed in Clyde, and feared he might soon return to his criminal past. Clyde visited Bonnie continually throughout the rest of February, and Mrs. Parker was visibly disturbed by his constant presence. She still had hopes of her beautiful daughter finding a man who would be a more stable person, and one who could bring happiness and security to the family without resorting to criminal behavior. Both the Parker and Barrow families were elated when Clyde's sister found her brother a job in Worcester, Massachusetts. There he could at least be away from his old criminal cronies for a while, and perhaps find a direction in life everyone could feel happy and comfortable about.

Clyde traveled to Massachusetts, and took the construction job that Nell had arranged for him. Less than two weeks later, however, he quit his job and returned to Dallas on March 17, 1932. He returned to his parents' Dallas home to find his sister furious over his abandoned attempt to handle a legitimate job. Nell had compromised her own integrity by pledging that Clyde had changed and could now handle the job to the employer's satisfaction. Clyde's only answer to Nell was that he had become so homesick for his family and Bonnie that he simply could not do his work there as expected.

"Times are hard and jobs hard to find, I know," Clyde exclaimed, "but I'll find a job to make you proud around here somewhere."

"I'll tell you this, Clyde Barrow," Nell answered, "you better not get involved ever again with that bunch you ran with before you went to the pen or you will end up dead for sure."

"Don't worry, sis. I've learned my lesson," Clyde replied to his sister.

⇥7⇤

THE BARROW GANG
IS FORMED

Bonnie, knowing how much her mother worried about her seeing Clyde and his friends, didn't tell Mrs. Parker when Clyde returned from New England. She decided to leave Dallas with Clyde, and explained to her mother she had been offered a good job with a cosmetic company in Houston demonstrating their facial make-up products.

"I can't find a job here, Mama, and you always wanted me to use my looks to get a job," Bonnie explained.

Clyde completely ignored the concerns and desires of his family and Bonnie and her family. He formed a gang, perhaps as a means to fight back against the terrible depression the country was facing. Among his first recruits was a Dallas bootlegger and auto thief, Raymond Hamilton. He also arranged for a McKinney, Texas, burglar, Ralph Fultz, to join them.

On April 19, 1932, Hamilton, Bonnie, and Clyde unsuccessfully tried to rob a store in Kaufman, Texas, before breaking into a hardware store there to obtain guns and ammunition. A night watchman set off an alarm that created an opportunity for what was to become only one of many fantastic getaways by the Barrow Gang.

Spring rains had turned the muddy dirt roads they followed from Kaufman into a quagmire, and the car was soon

Barrow Gang's associate Raymond Hamilton's prison photos. (Photo courtesy of Dallas Public Library)

buried to the axles in mud. With the police close behind, the three bandits tried to escape by running through adjacent fields in different directions. Clyde found some mules, caught one, and then helped Bonnie mount the animal before mounting another one himself. No matter how much they beat them, however, the mules refused to move, so they soon found themselves on foot again, running through the muddy fields.

Hamilton was captured. Clyde would have been shot or captured had the two officers pursuing them not stopped to reload their weapons. Clyde dropped Bonnie into a large culvert and told her he would return shortly, after finding transportation. A day and a half later, Clyde still had not returned, so she crawled to a nearby highway and began hitchhiking. The first driver to stop was, unfortunately, a posse member, who drove Bonnie directly to the Kaufman jail for questioning.

Bonnie admitted nothing. Hamilton had somehow escaped the jail before Bonnie was picked up. Bonnie's phone call to her mother and explanation as to how she ended up in the Kaufman jail, instead of being in Houston to begin an exciting new cosmetics career must have been either very creative or quite embarrassing for Bonnie. Mrs. Parker, fed up with her daughter's lies and disregard of her advice, decided not to try to bail Bonnie out of jail, and decided to leave her there for a while to once and for all teach her a much needed lesson.

While waiting for the grand jury to meet, Bonnie once again became disenchanted with Clyde. After all, he did not come back for her, and had left her in the field to be caught. Secondly, robbing small hardware stores was far from a glamorous lifestyle. Bonnie wanted, and thought, she deserved more in her life than this, and she certainly deserved a man who would show her more respect.

Clyde and Raymond Hamilton were loose and out robbing while Bonnie remained in a small town jail with no one trying to help get her out. During this depressing period, Bonnie wrote the following poem. It is obviously about Bonnie and the thoughts she was having as she waited for Clyde to come to her rescue.

"The Story of Bonnie and Clyde"
by Bonnie Parker

You have heard the story of Jesse James,
Of how he lived and died.
If you still are in need of something to read,
Here is the story of Bonnie and Clyde.

Now Bonnie and Clyde are the Barrow gang,
I'm sure you all have read
How they rob and steal,
And how those who squeal,
Are usually found dying or dead.

There are lots of untruths to their write-ups,
They are not so merciless as that;
They hate all the laws,
The stool-pigeons, spotters and rats.

If a policeman is killed in Dallas
And they have no clues to guide—
If they can't find a fiend,
They just wipe the slate clean,
And hang it on Bonnie and Clyde.

If they try to act like citizens,
And rent them a nice little flat,
About the third night they are invited to fight,
by a submachine gun rat-tat-tat.

A newsboy once said to his buddy;
"I wish old Clyde would get jumped;
"In these awful hard times,
"We'd make a few dimes
"If five or six cops would get bumped."

They class them as cold-blooded killers,
They say they are heartless and mean,
But I saw this with pride,
That once I knew Clyde
When he was honest and upright and clean.

But the law fooled around,
Kept tracking him down,
And locking him up in a cell,
Til he said to me,
"I will never be free,
So I will meet a few of them in hell."

This road was so dimly lighted.
There were no highway signs to guide,
But they made up their minds
If the roads were all blind
They wouldn't give up till they died.

The road gets dimmer and dimmer,
Sometimes you can hardly see,
Still it's fight man to man,
And do all you can,
For they know they can never be free.

They don't think they are too tough or desperate.
They know the law always wins.

They have been shot at before
But they do not ignore
That death is the wages of sin.

For heartbreaks some people have suffered,
From weariness some people have died,
But take it all and all,
Our troubles are small,
Till we get like Bonnie and Clyde.

Some day they will go down together;
And they will bury them side by side.
To a few it means grief,
To the law it's relief,
But it's death to Bonnie and Clyde.

While Bonnie continued to wait, Clyde and Raymond Hamilton joined up with another ex-convict, Frank Clause, and continued to commit crimes. During April 1932, they laid out plans for robbing the Bucher Store in Hillsboro, Texas. John and Martha Bucher had operated their small station and shop at the Highway 77 and 81 intersection near Hillsboro for many years.

John Bucher was inventorying stock in the store on the afternoon of April 30. Two employees, Marvin Kitchens and Bedell Jordan, were working in the front of the store. Shortly after 5:00 P.M., Clyde, Raymond, and Clause drove up to the Bucher store in a dark 1932 Ford sedan, got out of the car, and entered the shop.

Explaining that he wanted to look at watches, Raymond was guided to a display counter by one of the employees.

"These ain't good enough," Raymond shouted. "I want the best."

Jordan called Bucher from the back and told him what the customer was insisting on seeing. Mr. Bucher led the three men to his safe in the back, telling them that the safe was where his best watches were kept. The three men looked at the watches for some time, but they finally left without making a purchase.

That evening, around 10:30 P.M., Mr. and Mrs. Bucher, who lived in an apartment above the store, were awakened by someone beating on their back door. After trying to discourage the men and requesting unsuccessfully that they come back the next day, Mr. Bucher went down to open the store. The men explained that they were sent to buy some guitar strings by a band at the dance they were attending.

Mr. Bucher, hoping they would leave quickly, handed them the guitar strings. The robbers then pretended that they had no small change, only a large bill, requiring Bucher to open his safe for change. Bucher called his wife down, as his eyes were poor and he had difficulty working the safe combination.

Just as the safe door opened, Raymond Hamilton pulled a gun from his pocket and demanded that Bucher hand over the cash box and the other safe contents. Undoubtedly very nervous, Raymond's finger slipped, causing the gun to fire. The bullet hit the heavy safe door and ricocheted directly into Bucher's heart. Regrettably, the old man died instantly.

"It was an accident," Raymond replied when Clyde asked him what the hell he was doing. This was the group's first known killing, and though apparently not intentional, it greatly increased the recognition of, and the rewards for, the Barrow Gang.

Clyde was identified by Mrs. Bucher using police photo comparisons. Raymond Hamilton was also identified from the photos. Clyde realized that this was a turning point in his life—he could claim the death of Bucher was an accident and was not his doing and hope for a minor charge, or he could run for freedom. So run he did. Like a frightened animal, Clyde ran directly to his parents' home and hid in a drainage ditch behind the house. The next day, Clyde's sister Nell visited the Barrow home, where she interrogated her brother about the killing and his involvement.

"Yes, sis. It was an accident," Clyde explained. "I was just the driver."

Five days after the Bucher killing, Clyde came out of hiding to join up with Frank Clause in still another robbery scheme. On May 5, the two drove to Lufkin, Texas, where they stopped at a Magnolia station. After getting the attendant to fill their car with gas, both men walked into the station's office and waited for the attendant to enter. When he did, two guns were pointed at the man, and they demanded that he open the cash register and hand over all the money. Clyde and Frank then forced the attendant to get in the back seat of their car and go with them.

The men drove four blocks down to a Gulf station, where they forced the station manager to empty his cash drawer and join Clause and his hostage in the car. Clyde once again got behind the wheel and raced away. A short time later, Clyde and Clause released their two hostages, unharmed, on Highway 69 near Central Expressway.

During the months ahead, Clyde continued committing crimes around Dallas with Clause and Raymond Hamilton. Clyde often took refuge in an abandoned farmhouse near the Grand Prairie community in west Dallas while he waited for the Kaufman grand jury decision about Bonnie Parker's fate.

Bonnie's case was finally heard on June 17, 1932. The jury convinced the judge she should be released due to lack of evidence. Bonnie returned to her family home, and her mother noticed a major change in Bonnie's personality and conduct. Mrs. Parker made it clear—"If Clyde Barrow keeps up the way he is going, you have to stay away from him."

"You don't need to worry, Ma. I'm having nothing to do with him ever again," Bonnie pledged.

Soon afterward Mrs. Parker came home from work one evening to find that Bonnie had left for Wichita Falls, Texas, some two hundred miles northwest of Dallas, to apply for a waitress job in a new cafe scheduled to open soon. Naturally suspicious, Emma Parker was relieved when she received a letter from Bonnie about the wonderful new job and her nice apartment there. Bonnie's letter was entirely misleading, for both Clyde and Hamilton were living with Bonnie in a two-bedroom house. While Bonnie worked at her waitress duties, over the next several weeks Clyde and Hamilton managed to commit several small crimes throughout north Texas.

Bonnie had not seen her mother for several weeks and begged Clyde to take her back to Dallas to visit. Not expecting Clyde to be planning a robbery there, Bonnie left with Clyde for Dallas early on August 1, 1932. After he dropped her off at her mother's house, Clyde and Raymond picked up Everett Milligan, a newcomer to their circle of accomplices.

The *Dallas Morning News* reported that the Barrow Gang cruised around the Oak Cliff section of Dallas searching for another automobile to steal. Soon they spotted a desirable auto near the one hundred block of North Winnetka. Raymond jumped out and ran to a light colored sedan parked at the curb and soon had it started. The two cars then traveled together toward north Dallas as their drivers carefully observed all traffic laws. As they turned onto Alamo Street, Clyde pulled his car onto the shoulder, abandoned his car, and, along with Milligan, joined Hamilton in the light colored sedan.

Milligan slid behind the wheel around 4:00 P.M., and slowly drove into the parking lot of Newhoff Brothers Packing Company. The outlaws knew that employees of the firm were paid in cash around this time. Clyde and Hamilton, with guns drawn, entered the front door and proceeded into the main office. There, Elsie Wullschleger was found carefully counting the payroll cash. Joe and Henry Newhoff, owners of the company, were sitting at their desks in the rear of the office. Announcing his intentions, Clyde maneuvered to where he could cover all three, and Raymond Hamilton scooped up most of the cash in less than a minute. Following Hamilton down the hall, Clyde stopped briefly to yank the front office reception telephone from the wall. The men hurried to their waiting sedan, and Milligan raced away.

The men rushed to where they had left their original car on Alamo Street, changed vehicles, and, with Clyde now at the wheel, sped west to Industrial Boulevard and passed a police car occupied by a Captain A. F. Deere and Sergeant Roy Richburg, who were on their way outside the city limits for target practice. Noting Clyde's car as it sped passed them, the officers turned to follow. Clyde was driving at speeds exceeding seventy miles per hour and soon lost the pursuing police. Dozens of officers searched for the party widely throughout Dallas, but the robbers made a clean getaway. After eluding the officers in pursuit, Clyde hurriedly picked up Bonnie, and the four managed to hide out in an abandoned farmhouse near the Grand Prairie community in west Dallas for several days.

Several days later, on August 5, 1932, Clyde returned Bonnie to her mother's home for a few days while Raymond and Milligan drifted on to Corsicana, Texas, some eighty miles south of Dallas. Always staying one step ahead of the law, they managed to keep stealing cars and eluding capture. Eventually, they came back to pick up Clyde and head north to Oklahoma. Not trusting Raymond and Milligan's ability to keep ahead of the law, Clyde stopped in north Texas where Raymond stole still another car. Two more were later added to the list of cars stolen as the desperados fled Texas.

⊰8⊱

BEYOND TEXAS
AND BACK AGAIN

Crossing the Red River, the men used care to travel only the country roads, while continually looking for businesses they might burglarize. As usual, Clyde drove most of the time. Hamilton drank moonshine whiskey from a Mason jar quite frequently, and he occasionally let Milligan sample the spirits in the back seat.

One evening, while driving through the small community of Stringtown, Oklahoma, the group was drawn to a very crowded open-air dance pavilion. Clyde slowed the car and carefully surveyed the crowd at the dance and in the surrounding parking lot. Clyde tried to convince Hamilton, who desperately wanted to join the fun, that stopping might be dangerous. Finally, not being able to make them understand the danger, Clyde turned the car around and reluctantly pulled into the parking lot.

All three men entered the pavilion and enjoyed dancing and drinking with several of the local girls for a time. Feeling their welcome may be running out, they decided to leave the dance around 11:00 P.M., before any trouble began. Clyde and Hamilton left immediately for the car, while Milligan remained in deep conversation with an Oklahoma man. Hamilton, who continued to drink heavily, insisted

The Stringtown, Oklahoma, dance hall where two lawmen were killed by the Barrow Gang.

that Clyde join him in drinking, saying that Clyde needed to learn how to relax. Clyde, however, had learned many years before to use extreme caution in using alcohol because it affected his judgement. This was an especially good decision on this occasion, as he was soon challenged, and was required to leave the Stringtown dance rather quickly.

Prohibition was still in force at the time, and most Oklahoma officers strictly enforced the federal drinking laws and statutes. Sheriff C. G. Maxwell and Deputy E. C. Moore had observed Hamilton drinking from his fruit jar at the dance and followed the men as they left the party and returned to their vehicle.

"Consider yourselves under arrest, gentlemen," the officers told Clyde and Hamilton. Such a statement from strangers in a dark parking lot was not a wise one, and Hamilton and Clyde naturally pulled their pistols from their coats as they opened the car doors and opened fire. Deputy Moore died instantly from a mortal wound to the head, and Maxwell fell shortly afterward as a result of several wounds. Clyde instantly started the car and raced from the parking lot, with Hamilton swinging on an open door. Though severely wounded, Sheriff Maxwell managed to empty the chamber of his pistol into the fleeing vehicle.

Milligan, still dancing when the shooting began, suspected his friends might be involved, so he quietly merged into the heart of the anxious crowd on the dance floor. Later that evening, a new friend Milligan had made at the dance drove him into town, where he would escape the territory on a bus. Everett Milligan was not known to ever again associate with Clyde Barrow or Raymond Hamilton.

The few shots Clyde's car took from Maxwell's gun forced Clyde to lose control and swerve into a ditch a short distance from the dance. Cleve Brady noticed the car having problems, and slowed to offer assistance. Clyde immediately pulled his gun and demanded that Brady sit quietly while he took his car. Raymond got in the back seat. Clyde sped away to the northeast for some distance, but then Brady's car stalled. Clyde and Hamilton left Brady with his disabled car, found a small farmhouse, and awakened the farmer.

"I wrecked my car and need to get my injured friend to a doctor," Clyde told the farmer, John Redden. Redden, or perhaps his son, Lonnie, opened the door and took them to their car. Clyde took over the auto at gunpoint as Redden got in the back seat and Hamilton in the front, where he could better guard their hostage.

Speeding down back roads, the fugitives managed to travel to Clayton, Oklahoma, where another car was stolen from Frank Smith of Seminole, Oklahoma, who was visiting friends in Clayton. Clyde thanked Redden for his help, and left him standing by his car as Clyde and Hamilton sped off into the night in Smith's car.

Within a few hours of the Stringtown shooting, state investigators, sheriffs, and deputies from McAlister, Colgate, Antlers, and other communities in the region joined in the manhunt. Systematically questioning all the known witnesses, the lawmen learned that a third man had arrived with the party, but did not leave with the two that fled. They learned that a Stringtown man took this other man to the bus station that evening. A clerk at the bus depot remembered the excited passenger who bought a ticket for McKinney, Texas, and he told the officers that the bus left soon after the man came in. Texas authorities were notified, and Everett Milligan was arrested as he disembarked from the bus in McKinney.

While Oklahoma authorities were interrogating Milligan, Clyde and Hamilton had somehow slipped back into Texas and familiar territory. Traveling the back roads, the two soon reached Grandview, some thirty miles south of Fort Worth, Texas. Frank Smith's car was abandoned there, and another one was stolen to take them back to Dallas.

Bonnie was sitting on the porch visiting with her mother, Emma Parker, on the hot night of August 6, 1932. She was planning to leave for Wichita Falls the next day, as she felt she could find a better life there. It was around 8:00 P.M. when Raymond Hamilton pulled his car up to the front walk and signaled to Bonnie. Disregarding her mother's objections, Bonnie ran to the car, where she was told that Clyde was waiting for them at their Grand Prairie hideout.

Bonnie was then faced with a crucial moment of decision that would later prove to be the beginning of the folk saga of "Bonnie and Clyde," a story of two desperate lovers that has inspired volumes of literature (including this volume), for over sixty-five years. Looking back at her mother sitting in her rocker on the front porch, Bonnie asked Hamilton to wait a few minutes for her to tell her mother goodbye. She ran back to the house and told her mother that she loved her and had a ride to Wichita Falls, so she would not need the bus fare loaned to her earlier by Mrs. Parker. Placing the cash in her mother's lap and giving her mother a long and love-filled hug, Bonnie finally turned to accept the tragic life Clyde Barrow was now beckoning her to join, rejecting finally and totally the dreams Mrs. Parker had always had for her lovely daughter.

⇥9⇤

SOMETIMES
FALSELY ACCUSED

By this time, many crimes of all kinds throughout Texas, as well as mid-America, were being blamed on the notorious Barrow Gang. On October 11, 1932, Howard Hall, a butcher, was found murdered in his Sherman, Texas, meat shop. As usual, the Barrow Gang was blamed. Clyde, however, later told his family and associates that he had nothing whatsoever to do with this particular murder.

Soon after this Sherman accusation, Clyde added a youth named William Daniel (W. D. or "Deacon") Jones to the gang. They met at a Saturday night dance in the Fishtrap community of east Dallas. Clyde, Bonnie, and W. D. joined Raymond Hamilton in what would prove to be one of their bloodiest criminal joy rides in the annals of our nation's history.

W. D. not only became a trusted family friend, he also had no criminal record and so Clyde felt that he would be an asset. W. D. was naturally excited about becoming a part of the notorious Barrow Gang, regardless of the danger involved.

Shortly after he joined the group, W. D., Bonnie, and Clyde drove to Temple, Texas, on December 23, where they hoped to find a different vehicle. After spending the night in a tourist court there, the three began driving around the town looking for the right car to take. Finally, they spotted Clyde's favorite—a Ford Roadster—but neither W. D. nor Clyde could get the car started. A woman who noticed the activity ran from a house screaming, "Daddy, they are stealing your car!" As others ran out, Clyde drew his gun and told them all to step back if they expected to live. They all retreated, except one who ignored Clyde's threat, charged him, and began beating him. This courageous man was Doyle Johnson, a lumber salesman. Clyde shot at Johnson several times, but missed hitting him. W. D. Jones then turned and fired several rounds toward Johnson as well. Mr. Johnson was wounded very seriously, but recovered from his wounds, only to be killed a month later in Dallas.

W. D. had proven himself under pressure in Temple, and upon their return to Dallas, during the Christmas holidays of 1932, W. D. became a full-time member of the Barrow Gang. Before leaving the motel Christmas morning, Clyde gave Jones a .45 caliber pistol in case they ran into trouble shopping for still another V-8 Ford.

There were now four killings being blamed on the Barrow Gang, and Bonnie and Clyde were being blamed for almost all other crimes being committed throughout the country. The couple had no choice but to keep moving.

Many of Clyde's friends from the west Dallas campground began committing their own crimes, because they knew that whatever they did, Bonnie and Clyde would be blamed for it. For instance, only four days after Doyle Johnson was seriously injured, Clyde's friends since childhood, Odell Chambless and Les Stewart, walked into the Home Bank in Grapevine, Texas, only a short distance from the Barrow home, and took $3,000.00 at gunpoint. The robbery was blamed on the Barrow Gang, and police roadblocks were set up throughout the county.

Clyde, W. D., and Bonnie cautiously returned to Dallas on Friday, January 6, 1933. This visit would prove to be the catalyst that triggered the final episode in the romantic and exciting lives of Bonnie and Clyde.

Barrow Gang member W. D. (William Daniel) Jones, sometimes called "Deacon" Jones. (Photo courtesy of Dallas Public Library)

William Daniel (W. D.) Jones, Barrow Gang member with some of their weapons. (Photo courtesy of Marie Barrow Scoma)

❧10❧

ON THE RUN

Raymond Hamilton had been transferred to the Hillsboro, Texas, prison to stand trial for his part in the Bucher murder. Hamilton's sister, Lillie McBride, was living at 507 County Avenue, and often let her brother's friends take refuge there. Captured only a few hours after the Grapevine bank robbery, Les Stewart informed Dallas police that the McBride home often served as a safe house for the Barrow Gang. Stewart made a deal with the police and offered to set up a trap for Bonnie and Clyde in exchange for leniency for Stewart's part in the bank robbery.

When Bonnie and Clyde arrived back in Dallas, Bonnie begged to stop to see her mother at her home on Lamar Street. While Clyde and W. D. circled the block, Bonnie dashed in to hug her mother. Aware that her home was under constant surveillance by Dallas patrol cars, Mrs. Parker hysterically screamed for Bonnie to leave quickly before she was discovered.

After only a few minutes, Bonnie saw Clyde's car slowly passing the house, and she ran out to join him and W. D. The party of three had picked up a radio somewhere for their friend Raymond Hamilton. They also picked up a saw blade, which they then carefully hid inside the radio. After

Fugitive Raymond Hamilton with his mother. (Photo courtesy of Dallas Public Library)

The home of Lilly McBride near the Barrow garage in west Dallas where Bonnie, Clyde, and W. D. Jones had a gun battle with Texas lawmen. (Photo courtesy of Phillip Steele)

leaving Mrs. Parker's home, the three fugitives drove to the McBride home to give the radio and the message about the saw blade to Lillie McBride, hoping she could manage to deliver the items to her brother.

Unaware that Dallas lawmen and a Texas Ranger had staked out the McBride home hoping to capture the other Grapevine bank robber, Odell Chambless, Bonnie, Clyde, and W. D. slowly drove by the home around midnight. Finally deciding the house was safe, Clyde drove up in front and left the engine running. Clyde emerged from the car with a sawed off shotgun and slowly approached the house. Texas Ranger Van Noy first spotted Clyde approaching the house, and ran into the living room to notify the other officers waiting there. In a whisper, he quickly told them, "Get ready, boys. He is coming in with a sawed off shotgun!"

All the lights were out in the house, except for a small red light left on by Maggie Farrie, a friend of Lillie McBride who was staying in the home caring for Lillie's young son. As Clyde approached, he saw through the window the outline of Deputy Fred T. Bradberry, the largest of the officers waiting there. Not taking any chances, Clyde immediately fired his shotgun toward the shadow of Deputy Bradberry. Chaos immediately broke out as the three other officers returned fire. W. D., still in the car with Bonnie, grabbed a shotgun and fired toward the house through the window. Bonnie grabbed him because she was afraid he might accidentally hit Clyde in the dark.

Deputies Walter Evans and Malcolm Davis had been watching the back of the house when the firing began, and they ran around the house just in time to get a glimpse of Clyde as he retreated from the front porch. Seeing the deputies' shadows, Clyde turned toward Deputy Davis and let him have a second charge from his shotgun.

As was the case in almost all of Clyde's escapades that involved shooting, Clyde didn't intend to wound these lawmen. Clyde shot to kill. Evans dropped to the ground with his chest and stomach full of buckshot. Evans managed to get off several rounds from his pistol, but none hit Clyde as he ran to the parked Ford. Evans was rushed to Methodist Hospital, where doctors pronounced him dead upon arrival.

Bonnie saw Clyde running and drove to pick him up. Halting the car, she let Clyde slide behind the steering wheel, while W. D. remained in the front passenger seat. Clyde wasted no time speeding past Westmoreland Street onto Industrial Boulevard, where he turned south as fast as the Ford would go. After escaping the Dallas turmoil, Clyde turned the car northeast toward Sherman at about 1:00 A.M. He kept the accelerator to the floor as he remained slumped over the wheel, stopping only for food and gasoline. By dawn they had reached central Oklahoma, where they found a tourist cabin to rent. They stayed there for two weeks for a badly needed rest.

It may have been sometime during those two weeks that Bonnie and Clyde visited Bradley and Charles Arthur ("Pretty Boy") Floyd at his oil field bungalow in Seminole, Oklahoma. Most who have written about Bonnie and Clyde have not indicated any connection between the couple and Pretty Boy Floyd; however, the following statement of Bradley Floyd, Pretty Boy's brother, in Sallisaw, Oklahoma, recorded in 1974, seems to have been told with sincerity:

"Bonnie brought this cute little white dog with her when they came, and we were afraid all the dogs barking would bring all of us unneeded attention. . . . We knew Clyde briefly from following the wheat harvest in Kansas one year and kept up with their newspaper stories, but were not what you call good friends."

Now somewhat rested and relaxed, Clyde, Bonnie, and W. D. leisurely traveled eastward, making sure they remained within the speed limits, as they certainly could not afford being stopped for a simple traffic violation. On the night of January 31, 1933, however, Thomas Persell, a Springfield, Missouri, motorcycle policeman started chasing Clyde's car just as they were crossing a bridge. Clyde had always feared bridges due to the fact that roadblocks could easily prevent escape when they were set up on a bridge.

"Pull over, sir," the policeman commanded as he pulled up along Clyde's left side.

"Just a minute, sir," Clyde responded, as he continued over the bridge.

Apparently, Persell became very angry when Clyde refused to stop until he had crossed the bridge and then pulled into a dark street. Persell parked his motorcycle and approached Clyde's car as he asked, "Where are you going in such a rush?"

The traffic policeman was undoubtedly shocked when Clyde raised his sawed off shotgun from his lap and pointed it directly in Persell's face. Jones then jumped out, walked around the car with his pistol drawn, and disarmed Persell. Clyde and W. D. forced Persell to get into the back seat of the car, where W. D. covered him with a blanket and climbed in next to him as Clyde slowly drove away. Thirty minutes or so later, a passing vehicle noticed the abandoned motorcycle and became suspicious. A major manhunt was soon underway throughout the entire region.

Fully realizing that they were being aggressively sought by the authorities throughout the country, and fearing capture at any time, the outlaws avoided using major highway routes as much as possible, and they traded cars as often as convenient. Car license plates were also changed frequently. Their screwdriver was used perhaps even more than their guns, as they could remove license plates from a parked vehicle quickly and exchange the stolen one with their own car plate in a matter of seconds.

The group kept Persell with them while Clyde followed a twisting route through the southwestern Missouri Ozarks. Visiting Buffalo, Golden City, Carthage, Fairplay, Orogono, and other small communities, the foursome soon became bored—if indeed that was possible for this party. When they stopped briefly in Orogono, the car battery would not start their car when they were ready to leave. Clyde requested that W. D. walk into town and steal a battery. W. D. persuaded Clyde that Officer Persell should go along to carry the battery. Persell had guessed by this time who his kidnappers were, and undoubtedly expected to be killed by them. W. D. and Persell were soon back with a new battery. Once the car was started and ready to go, Clyde told Persell not to get into the car. The thankful and surprised Persell had to have been relieved as Clyde drove off into the night.

Just where they traveled over the next several weeks of the Ozark winter is not certain. Perhaps the only clue to their activities during this period comes from the folklore still being told about their visits to such Ozark tourist resorts as Lake Lucerne in Eureka Springs, Arkansas, Noel in southwest Missouri, Winslow and Monte Ne in northwest Arkansas, and Hot Springs, Arkansas, where they are purported to have enjoyed mineral baths and gambling.

Traveling was expensive, and although the Barrow Gang took gas and automobiles as needed, food and lodging required considerable ingenuity so that they didn't alert the hundreds of lawmen they suspected were now on their trail. Living on the edge day and night took its toll on the three, and emotions swelled within them. It would seem very possible that they may have been asking themselves, *Is this really the life I want to live?*

✤11✤

BACK TO THE FOLD

On March 22, 1933, Buck Barrow, Clyde's older brother, was paroled from Texas State Prison. Buck's wife Blanche had been successful in getting her husband to surrender and return to prison after his escape. Now that Buck had paid his debt to society, she sincerely hoped that he would never again participate in unlawful activities. Buck had never liked guns, and his only crimes had been (primarily) petty theft. Blanche was surely hopeful that Buck would now share her desire to lead a clean life and build a future for the two of them.

Buck Barrow had been extremely concerned throughout his life about Clyde, and he felt somehow responsible for his younger brother becoming such a hardened criminal. As could be expected, the Barrow family hoped Buck would stay away from Clyde and his associates, for fear the gang might lure him into an unlawful and dangerous future. They were all, therefore, disappointed when Buck announced less than a week after his parole that he "wanted to see Clyde."

Buck by no means desired to follow Clyde's criminal ways, but he harbored the hope that he and their mother could succeed in getting Clyde to surrender to the authorities. If

Clyde were to take such a course, Buck thought it would go far in getting Clyde's many criminal charges dismissed or suspended. Most of the murder charges against Clyde were circumstantial or had been committed while running from lawmen. Buck therefore felt Clyde was probably tired enough of running and narrow escapes that he would be ready to listen to his big brother's advice.

Buck planned to take Blanche to visit her parents in Missouri, and Buck's sister, Nell, had even gone so far as to purchase a car for Buck to prevent any possible suspicions that the car had been stolen. Blanche and her family suggested that Buck consider settling down on their Missouri farm and becoming a respectable citizen. Buck, however, was determined to see Clyde before he would make any plans for his own future.

Somehow Buck made arrangements for a rendezvous with Clyde through the brothers' west Dallas contact, Floyd Hamilton. Blanche cried the entire trip, partially from fear, and certainly because Buck rejected her wishes for them. Buck drove from his parents' home in Dallas to Fort Smith, Arkansas, where the brothers met and further discussed reunion plans. They left Fort Smith and drove north on U.S. Highway 71 to Joplin, Missouri, where they rented a two-story stone bungalow garage apartment at 3347½ 34th Street in the Freeman Park subdivision of south Joplin. Paul Freeman, owner of the apartments, had been approached by two women and a man on April 1, 1933. One of the women told Freeman that her husband, W. L. Callahan, was a visiting engineer from Minnesota. Clyde's Ford V-8 and a Ford coupe were parked in the apartment garages.

Clyde had been very selective in choosing the bungalow location. Not only was the city of Joplin considered to be a "safe" city for gangsters during that period, the bungalow offered a quick escape since it was within one hundred yards of a north and south major paved highway, and there were two garages below the five-room apartment.

The famous photo of Bonnie and Clyde clowning near Joplin, Missouri. (Photo courtesy of Marie Barrow Scoma)

The notorious Bonnie Parker smoking a cigar and holding a gun while clowning near Joplin, Missouri. (Photo courtesy of Marie Barrow Scoma)

Clyde (left) and Buck Barrow. (Photo courtesy of Marie Barrow Scoma)

The Joplin, Missouri, apart-ments where the Barrow Gang had a shootout with Joplin lawmen. (Photo cour-tesy of Phillip Steele)

Buck rented another garage under the name of Callahan nearby at 3339 Oak Street for his 1929 Marmon sedan. This garage was owned by Sam Langford.

The long anticipated reunion of the brothers apparently went well. Buck brought family news to Bonnie and Clyde. While the brothers visited, Bonnie rested and caught up on the latest Hollywood news by reading and re-reading all the movie and romance magazines she could find. Bonnie and Blanche shared cooking, and Bonnie enjoyed making her specialty of red beans and cabbage.

Clyde Barrow holding a Browning Automatic Rifle taken during the robbery of the National Guard. (Photo courtesy of Marie Barrow Scoma) (The photo was no doubt taken by Bonnie Parker, as a copy of one such photo was found in Joplin, Missouri.)

Neighbors began to notice that the two Fords at the apartment were seldom used, and that the sedan parked in the Langford garage down the street was usually the only one any of the renters drove. Generally, the group enjoyed the simple pleasures: talking, playing cards, eating, and drinking beer. After two weeks or so, though, their funds began to run low. Later reports indicated that they were down to their last $8.00.

Clyde, without consulting Buck, along with W. D. Jones, began seeking out locations suitable for robbing. Neighbors became more and more anxious and disturbed by these strangers. Not only were their loud radio music and late parties of some concern, several became suspicious when a large number of license plates were seen in the garage when it was open for a while. Others had seen firearms being carried into the apartment. Joplin was noted for its acceptance of border bootlegging and whiskey-running operations, so most of the residents in the area simply thought the Barrows must be involved in similar activities. A few of the neighbors, however, became so concerned that the Joplin police were called in to help with a search warrant for the apartment.

On Thursday, April 13, 1933, Clyde had decided it was time for him and W. D. to go out on another scouting trip. The sixth sense that Clyde Barrow seems to have always had when danger was near evidently warned him on this day, because he and W. D. returned to the apartment earlier than planned. At 4:00 P.M. Clyde pulled the car into the garage and lowered the door. Upstairs, Bonnie was cooking her normal red beans and cabbage, while Blanche played solitaire and Buck slept with Blanche's dog.

Joplin Detective Tom DeGraff, New County Constable John W. Harryman, and Joplin Motor Car Detective Harry McGinnis all drove up in front of the apartment in one car, driven by DeGraff. Seeing that one of the garage doors was partly open, DeGraff drove the car straight up to the door. As the police car bumped the door, someone inside tried to close it. Officer Harryman slipped out of the police car, ran to the garage door, and attempted to raise it. As he did so, a sawed off shotgun stuck beneath the door was fired blindly. Harryman took the full charge, and fell, mortally wounded, to the garage floor as the door opened.

Detective Harry McGinnis had jumped from the rear seat as the car entered the driveway. McGinnis had his pistol in hand, but one of the Barrows fired a volley of gunshots that almost severed McGinnis's right arm. He was also hit with four shotgun blasts in the stomach and left side of his face. Crouching beside the car, Officer DeGraff fired his revolver at the garage windows repeatedly before running to the apartment's west wall.

Missouri State Trooper George Kahler had been alerted to the situation and parked on the west side of the apartment when he arrived at the scene. Trooper Grammer was with him, and immediately left the police car and ran to the west side of the structure. Kahler was soon out of the car and ran into the garage as one of the Barrows fired several shots at him before retreating into the building. Trooper Grammer realized the need for reinforcements, and ran to a neighbor's residence to call the station for more men. One of the gunmen suddenly ran out and released the brake on the police car, causing it to coast backwards across the street and away from the garage.

Clyde, sawed off shotgun in hand, grabbed Bonnie and half dragged her down the stairs to the garage and threw her into the car as Buck followed. Blanche was now screaming hysterically as she ran from the garage and down the sidewalk chasing her dog to the east. Clyde smashed the V-8 Ford through the half-open door and across the street into the police car, turned east, and sped toward Main Street, stopping only long enough for Buck to run down the screaming Blanche and put her in the car so they could speed away.

From personal items and photos found in the apartment and garage, authorities took little time identifying the mysterious renters as Clyde Barrow and Buck Barrow, Bonnie Parker, and Blanche Barrow. W. D. Jones was not identified

Buck Barrow's wife, Blanche. (Photo courtesy of Marie Barrow Scoma)

until several months later. One of Clyde's stolen V-8s was left in the apartment garage, and Buck's Marmon sedan was left in the Langford garage nearby. Authorities found it was owned by Buck, and had been purchased legally from a Carl Beaty. This was the car Buck's sister, Nell, personally bought for Buck when he was pardoned.

The scene left behind as the Barrows escaped was bloody carnage. Constable Wes Harryman had died, and lay in the driveway. Detective McGinnis's left arm had been blown away in the fracas, and he died later that evening in the hospital. Officer Tom DeGraff and Trooper George Kahler were both wounded badly, but they survived.

Texas Sheriff Smoot Schmit immediately sent Deputy Bob Alcorn to Joplin to review the evidence. Alcorn had been the chief investigator on many of the crimes credited to the Barrows. Alcorn asked to take Deputy Ted Hinton along, since he was also familiar with the Barrows.

Of all of the evidence found there, the two rolls of film proved to be the most valuable. Through interviews with various west Dallas gangsters, the identity of W. D. Jones became known for the first time. W. D. had been spotted during the murder of Doyle Johnson in Temple, Texas; at the killing of Deputy Malcolm Davis in west Dallas; and the kidnapping of Motorcycle Officer Thomas Persell in Springfield, Missouri. Now he could be positively identified.

Perhaps the most popular photos found in the apartment, and the ones that helped create many of the myths and mysteries about Bonnie and Clyde, was the series of photos showing Bonnie holding a revolver with a cigar in her mouth.

The press expanded upon the legend of Clyde's now infamous partner by publishing those photos in nationally syndicated news columns, calling Bonnie, "The cigar-smoking female gun mall." Bonnie was so insulted by these demeaning photos that she wrote a letter to various newspapers stating she did not smoke cigars, her preference being Camel cigarettes.

One of the weapons found in the apartment was a Browning Automatic Rifle, one of a number obtained by the Barrows during several robberies of various National Guard armories. The Browning Automatic Rifle (BAR) was Clyde's weapon of choice. A shoulder-fired light machine gun, the BAR weighted in at 16 pounds and was rather large and clumsy, but extremely powerful. The gun fired a high velocity .30 caliber metal-jacketed bullet, capable of penetrating $\frac{1}{2}$" of plate steel. The weapon had a cyclic rate of fire of 550 rounds per minute, but was difficult to master as the powerful 30-06 cartridge produced a forceful recoil. Clyde Barrow was so enamored with the weapon that he took every available moment to practice firing the big rifle. He became quite proficient with the BAR.

Other items found in the apartments included a sawed-off shotgun, a revolver, and five diamonds. Officers traced the diamonds to a jewelry store robbery that had taken place the previous day in Neosho, Missouri.

Texas authorities Alcorn and Hinton traveled to Joplin to help confirm that the Barrow Gang had indeed been there, and to credit still two more deaths to the now infamous gang. While Alcorn and Hinton were doing their work in Joplin, the Barrows were racing back to Texas. They continued to avoid major roadblocks in Kansas, Oklahoma, and Texas, before arriving in Amarillo about eight hours after leaving Joplin. In Amarillo, they finally stopped for their first rest, and to find medical attention for W. D., who had received a head wound in the Joplin shootout.

According to several accounts of the Barrow brothers, Clyde and Buck had been accused of being responsible, directly or indirectly, with the deaths of six men, four of whom had been police officers. Rewards for their capture increased dramatically, and, as a result of the Joplin photos, their faces were now known throughout the Southwest.

On the morning of April 27, 1933, the Barrows arrived in Ruston, Louisiana, Bonnie by Clyde's side in the front, and Buck, W. D., and Blanche crowded into the back seat. Clyde slowly surveyed this beautiful old Southern city, carefully noting the best escape routes if one became necessary.

It was time for them to pick up another car. H. Dillard Darby had left his new Chevrolet parked outside of his boarding house when he went home for lunch. As was customary in most small Southern towns of the time, Darby had left the keys in the car.

As these accounts of Bonnie and Clyde clearly indicate, Clyde Barrow greatly preferred the Ford V-8 to all the other types of automobiles. In fact, Clyde so loved the Ford he decided to write a personal letter pointing out the car's virtues to none other than Henry Ford himself. That letter says:

10th April
Mr. Henry Ford
Detroit, Mich.

Dear Sir: —

While I still have got breath in my lungs I will tell you what a dandy car you make. I have drove Fords exclusively when I could get away with one. For sustained speed and freedom from trouble the Ford has got ever other car skinned and even if my business haven't been strickly legal it don't hurt enything to tell you what a fine car you got in the V8 —

Yours truly
Clyde Champion Barrow
(Courtesy of the Marie Barrow Scoma collection)

This letter, written to Henry Ford, and signed by Clyde Barrow, appeared in newspapers throughout the nation. Marie Barrow said the letter was a fake since the handwriting does not match that of Clyde Barrow. Also, Clyde's middle name was Chestnut, not Champion, as shown here. (Photo courtesy of Marie Barrow Scoma)

Tulsa Okla
10th April

Mr Henry Ford
Detroit Mich.

RECEIVED
APRIL 14 1934
Dearborn, Mich.

Dear Sir:—
 While I still have got breath in my lungs I will tell you what a dandy car you make. I have drove Fords exclusivly when I could get away with one. For sustained speed and freedom from trouble the Ford has got ever other car skinned and even if my business havent been strickly legal it dont hurt enything to tell you what a fine car you got in the V8 —

Yours truly
Clyde Champion Barrow

This authentic reproduction of Clyde Barrow's handwritten letter is from the Ford Archives, Henry Ford Museum, Dearborn, Michigan. On May 25 —only slightly more than a month after the receipt of this letter—Clyde Chestnut Barrow (his middle name was not "Champion" as he insisted on signing his letters) and Bonnie Parker were ambushed and killed on a lonely dirt road between Gibsland and Sailes in Louisiana.

— Compliments of Helm/Lary Ford —

This letter, supposedly written to Henry Ford and signed by Clyde Barrow, appeared in newspapers throughout the nation. An authentic reproduction of the letter is kept in the Ford Archives, Henry Ford Museum, Dearborn, Michigan.

When the letter supposedly written by Clyde was published in newspapers throughout the country, it quite naturally boosted Ford Motor Company's sales, even during this economically depressed period.

In spite of his Ford preference, Clyde Barrow slowly drove by the boarding house and selected the parked Chevrolet belonging to Mr. Darby. He asked W. D. to jump out and start the Chevy while he circled the block. Since the keys were in it, it took W. D. only seconds to start the car. Bonnie and Clyde joined W. D. in the Chevrolet and drove off while the dumbfounded Darby, resting on the boarding house

Blanche Barrow (Buck's wife) with her father-in-law, H. B. Barrow. (Photo courtesy of Marie Barrow Scoma)

porch after lunch, watched his car move away. Darby ran from the porch and chased the car down the street before yelling back to those on the porch to call the authorities. Darby borrowed a car from Sophia Stone, a home demonstration agent for Lincoln Parish, Louisiana, who also had walked to the porch as the Darby car was being stolen. Sophia enthusiastically ran to her car with Darby, and they both got in and began chasing the Barrows. Darby and Stone dropped back, though, when it became apparent they could not possibly catch W. D. at the speed with which he was pushing Darby's new Chevrolet.

The Barrows proceeded down the Ruston-to-El Dorado, Arkansas, highway until barricades were seen. W. D. turned west onto the Hico Road and soon slowed the car and pulled off the road to wait for Darby and Stone to catch up with them. Clyde Barrow left the car and stood by the road signaling Darby to stop. Thinking Clyde was someone he knew, Darby pulled over to offer his assistance. As he did, Clyde quickly removed Darby and Stone from the vehicle and forced them to get into the Chevrolet with Bonnie, W. D., Blanche, and Buck before proceeding down the highway.

A cotton farmer witnessed the kidnapping and saw the bandits driving away, and he notified the authorities by telephone. Before the lawmen arrived in the area to begin a wide search for Darby and Stone, Clyde had turned the vehicle onto a gravel road leading to Bernice, Louisiana. Before stopping to get gasoline, Clyde instructed their captives, "If you don't keep quiet, I'll kill you and everybody at the gas station."

The Barrows and their back seat hostages arrived in El Dorado, Arkansas, and stopped for gas and oil. After walking around the car, they got back in and explained to their captives, "Well, we have decided not to kill you. We will let you go soon."

As their conversation became more casual, Bonnie asked them what they did for a living.

"I'm a home demonstration agent for the county," Ms. Stone explained.

Obviously slower in his response when he was asked his occupation, Darby answered, "I'm an undertaker."

Laughing, Bonnie stated, "When the law finally catches us, maybe you can fix us up. If they ever take us, though, we'll get the electric chair, so we probably won't need any undertaker," Bonnie announced as she squeezed Clyde's arm.

Clyde kept driving through south Arkansas. Magnolia, Waldo, and Prescott were on their route. Finally Clyde stopped some five miles out of town, a place from where it would take at least an hour to get to a phone, and he let his two hostages out of the car. As the car pulled away, it stopped suddenly and backed up to where the scared but relieved couple stood. When Buck Barrow got out and began walking toward the couple, both Stone and Darby surely must have felt that their lives on this earth were about to end. Then Buck handed Darby a $5.00 bill and said, "Maybe this will help you get back home."

The relieved couple found a man along the road who was changing a flat tire, and he agreed to drive them back to Waldo for $5.00. The authorities were out of town, but Darby and Stone got Waldo's mayor to drive them to Magnolia where Darby had a brother-in-law, Nick Mialos. They were soon on their way back to Ruston. Darby's car was found undamaged several days later near McGehee, Arkansas. From descriptions given by Darby and Stone when they returned, it was decided that the outlaws were the Barrow Gang.

⊰12⊱

FAMILY BONDS

A bus pulled into the Dallas terminal on Jackson Street on May 3, 1933. One of the passengers was very nervous, and probably very frustrated over the path her life had taken, so suddenly, over the past few weeks. This person was none other than Blanche Barrow. Blanche had never been in any kind of trouble in her life until those dreadful few minutes in Joplin, Missouri, when all that changed. Hurriedly walking through the terminal with her head lowered, Blanche flagged down a taxi, and gave the driver the address of Henry Barrow's shop. Blanche paid the driver and ran into the building, afraid that someone might be watching her.

Mrs. Barrow was understandably glad to see Blanche, and to learn that her two boys were still alive and well, although by then they were on the FBI's Most Wanted List. Blanche had brought the message that the outlaws wanted to see their families, and wanted to schedule a brief visit. Blanche had a map to guide the family to a prearranged site on a country road near a bridge around the Commerce community, about sixty miles northeast of Dallas.

Mrs. Barrow notified her daughter, Nell, as well as Bonnie's mother. According to Mrs. Barrow's diary, the family expected their telephone had been tapped by Texas authorities, so a code was set up to use when it was time to leave for a family rendezvous. "I'm cooking pinto beans for supper. Why don't you all come over?" was the signal, and it apparently worked.

Everyone enjoyed the family visit. It had been several months since they had been together, but a cloud of sadness and despair seemed to hover over the picnic. Everyone suspected it would not be long until their loved ones would be captured or shot to pieces by pursuing lawmen. Nell later said the meeting could be compared to that of visiting relatives on death row in prison.

Bonnie and Clyde freely discussed the charges of killing Malcolm Davis in Dallas, Doyle Johnson in Temple, of kidnapping Persell in Missouri, the Johns kidnapping in New Mexico, and the Stone-Darby kidnapping in Louisiana. Not unexpectedly, they denied having a part in dozens of other crimes blamed on them by newspapers and various lawmen.

Bonnie and her mother walked away from the crowd for the private conversation expected from and by any mother.

"Honey, try to find a way to leave Clyde and give up to the law," she pleaded. "A prison sentence is a great deal better than the certain death Clyde will lead you to."

"We both know Clyde will be killed, Mama. Clyde will never give up. When he dies, Mama, I will not have a reason to keep living, so I want to go with him," Bonnie confided to her mother.

The tearful parting came around dusk, with the families returning to Dallas and the outlaws back on the road toward Oklahoma. They drove on into Missouri, where Buck and Blanche stopped to visit Blanche's relatives near Caldwell in Missouri. Buck had actually planned to take up farming there upon his release from prison, and perhaps even raise a family, but now this option was gone forever, especially after the Joplin disaster.

Bonnie Parker and Clyde Barrow at a family rendezvous near Dallas. (Photo courtesy of Dallas Public Library)

Clyde Barrow's mother, Cumie Barrow (left), and Bonnie Parker's mother, Emma Parker (right), heartbroken mothers during one of the family meetings near Dallas. (Photo courtesy of Marie Barrow Scoma)

❈13❈

BAD MATTERS JUST
GOT WORSE

Raymond Hamilton's trial in LaGrange, Texas, for bank robbery, was scheduled to begin a short time after the Barrow/Parker reunion. The officers responsible for Hamilton's arrest returned him to Hillsboro on May 13, 1933, to begin serving his time. Shortly afterward, a witness in Hamilton's trial, Marvin Kitchens, was kidnapped in Hillsboro. Walking along Walton Street, Kitchens saw a man walking toward him. Just as he passed, the man whirled around and held a gun to Kitchens's back. An auto drove up, and Kitchens was forced into the car by the gunman. Warning Kitchens that he should be more careful about what he saw and did in the future, the kidnappers bound his hands and feet with wire before throwing him out of the car and racing away.

The jury in Hamilton's trial found him guilty; however, the jurors confronted difficulties agreeing on his sentence, and eventually a mistrial was declared. A new trial was then planned, but this time for the murder of John Bucher. This time the jury had little difficulty with the testimony, and by 9:30 A.M. on Friday, June 2, 1933, they had found Hamilton guilty of murder with malice, and sentenced him to another life term.

Several days after the Kitchens kidnapping incident on June 10, 1933, in Hillsboro, Bonnie and Clyde, and their trusted friend, W. D. Jones, who had rejoined his friends, were speeding down Texas Highway 203 between the communities of Quail and Wellington. Buck and Blanche were wearing out their welcome with Blanche's relatives in Missouri, but had not, as yet, left there. Six miles east of Wellington, a bridge over a large ravine had been taken out by a construction crew, but proper warning signs had not been erected. Driving at his usual seventy miles per hour, Clyde suddenly crashed over the edge of the ravine, causing the vehicle to roll over several times before landing on its top.

Bonnie was thrown from the car and pinned under it. Miraculously, the untouchable Clyde Barrow walked away unhurt. He first pulled W. D. loose, and got all the guns and ammo from the vehicle. Bonnie had been dazed, but soon regained consciousness and screamed for Clyde. Clyde and W. D. tried to lift the car, but it was too heavy for the two. Gasoline began to drip from the tilted tank, and a spark from somewhere suddenly ignited the fuel.

The gasoline trickled down across her legs, and soon Bonnie felt the flames follow. Her nylon stockings melted to her skin, and flames singed her hair and blisters formed on her face. She desperately struggled, but to no avail. She began to beg W. D. and Clyde to do something, anything. Together they pushed, but the vehicle was getting too hot to touch. At the most desperate moment, help arrived in the form of two farmers, Tom Pritchard and his neighbor, John Cartwright. They joined in, and the four men together lifted the car enough so that Clyde could pull Bonnie free. She was still on fire, and the men began to scoop up sand and dirt to smother the flames on her body.

Bonnie had been horribly burned. Her legs were most affected. The skin had burned away, revealing charred flesh, with the bone showing in two areas of one leg. Clyde gently lifted her, but she could not stop crying out at any movement or touch to the exposed flesh.

The farmers were immediately suspicious of the large cache of ammunition and weapons removed from the wrecked automobile. Clyde carried Bonnie up the hill to the Pritchard's farm. Mrs. Pritchard directed Clyde to the bedroom, and Bonnie was laid on clean sheets. Mrs. Pritchard washed and bandaged the wounds, then explained to Clyde the seriousness of the injuries. She insisted that Bonnie needed to go to a hospital and be under a doctor's care, because the extent of the burns would require skilled medical treatment.

When attentions were drawn away from him, John Cartwright slipped out the door, ran down the road to his own home, and telephoned the sheriff.

W. D. pointed a shotgun at the Pritchards while Clyde attempted to thank them for their help.

"I don't know what to do about moving you, Honey," Clyde told Bonnie.

"I can travel!" Bonnie exclaimed. "It will hurt terribly, I know, but we can't stay here," she further argued.

W. D.'s nerves were on edge because of all the trouble the wreck had caused, and he was trembling all over. The Pritchards were scared for their lives. Seizing the opportunity to escape, Mrs. Pritchard ran from the room when she saw Clyde look away. W. D. fired a shotgun through the door and injured Mrs. Pritchard's hand slightly.

"That is no way to treat someone trying to help us," the quite rattled Clyde shouted at W. D. Clyde knew they needed to find a car and leave the scene as soon as possible, before lawmen arrived. Apparently, neither Pritchard nor his neighbor owned a car.

Someone drove up to the house, and the three friends in crime left the house and hid behind a hedge in the yard. Sheriff Corry and the Wellington Town Marshal Tom Hardy stepped out of their cars. As the two men entered the house with guns drawn, Clyde and W. D. stepped in behind them and removed their weapons. They then bound the men with their own handcuffs. Clyde forced Marshal Hardy to get in

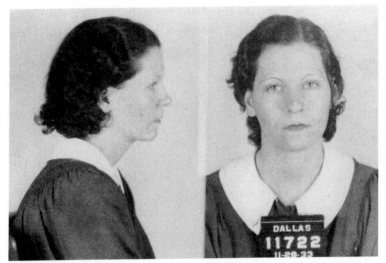

Billie Parker, Bonnie's sister, came to Fort Smith, Arkansas, to nurse Bonnie's burn wounds. (Photo courtesy of Marie Barrow Scoma)]

the back seat of his car and hold Bonnie on his lap. Corry was forced into the front seat with W. D. and Clyde, and they sped away toward Wellington.

Bonnie moaned constantly from the excruciating pain of her burns throughout the three-hour trip to reach Buck and Blanche, who were meeting them near Erick, Oklahoma. Finally, after a tragedy-filled day, Clyde pulled up alongside Buck's auto near Erick. Clyde ordered their two lawmen hostages out of the car and told them to walk to a nearby fence where their handcuffs were tied to the fence with fencing wire W. D. had cut out of the fence. Clyde and Buck contemplated killing the two officers to prevent future arrests, but Clyde commented, "They treated Bonnie pretty well, so I guess we'll let them live."

Blanche did what she could to comfort Bonnie and tend to her wounds. After putting her in Buck's car and loading up W. D., Blanche, and Buck, Clyde once more took the driver's seat. Corry and Hardy eventually freed their hands and were able to notify the authorities that the Barrow Gang was traveling east from Erick, Oklahoma. Although the alarm spread quickly, Clyde was yet again able to slip through the lawmen's net and drive on to Fort Smith, Arkansas, where they rented two cabins at the Dennis Tourist Courts on Midland Avenue.

Bonnie's burns needed nursing attention only a family member could properly provide, so on June 11, Clyde left for Dallas, where he wasted no time picking up Bonnie's sister, Billie, and returning to Fort Smith. Clyde and Billie arrived around dawn on June 12, 1933. Reports indicate that Bonnie was so delirious from pain that three days passed before she finally recognized her sister.

The closeness of six people sharing two small courts was by now getting on everyone's nerves, especially given Bonnie's constant moaning. Funds for food, medicine, ammunition, and rent were exhausted. The Dennis family, owners of the tourist court in Ft, Smith, had been told by the group that they were involved in a car accident that had caused Bonnie's terrible burns. This writer had occasion to interview a son of the Dennis family a few years ago, and he indicated that his parents and his sister definitely knew the identity of the Barrow Gang, and helped them with money, food, and medical supplies without notifying the authorities. In fact, the Barrows probably would not have survived as long as they did had not the Dennis family assisted them in this way. The Dennis daughter also arranged for a Fort Smith medical doctor to treat Bonnie, and the doctor also evidently kept his suspicions to himself. Even with the outside assistance, though, funds were extremely low, and Clyde suggested that W. D. and Buck seek out a source of money.

Bonnie Parker's sister, Billie Parker. (Photo courtesy of Dallas Public Library)

The Dennis Motel in Fort Smith, Arkansas, where Bonnie recuperated from her severe leg burns. (Photo courtesy of Phillip W. Steele)

◄14►

A BIT OF TIME
IN ARKANSAS

Fayetteville, Arkansas, sixty miles north of Fort Smith on
U.S. Highway 71, the county seat of Washington County,
and home of the University of Arkansas, was a very busy
community. On the way north, W. D. and Buck camped out
in a remote area south of Fayetteville and, on the morning
of June 23, drove into the city. They first drove around the
square, looking for a source of easy cash. The square was
bustling with activity, so they proceeded around the corner
to Dickson Street, and began to survey various isolated
stores and shops.

Buck slowly idled along the street as W. D. entered King's
Grocery and walked up and down the aisles. He soon left
and proceeded to Bates' Brothers Grocery. Mr. Bates
watched as the young man entered the store, walked the
aisles, and left without a purchase. A Ford car followed
along the road beside the short, squatty young man, and Mr.
Bates noted with suspicion their progress as they rounded
another corner onto Lafayette Street.

At 111 Lafayette, W. D. found what he had been looking
for. Located in a quiet residential area across from an ele-
mentary school stood a single-story brick structure, the
neighborhood market known as Brown's Grocery. Built in
1924, the business was owned and operated by Robert L.

and Nell Brown. Mr. Brown was away most of the time, as he had been appointed tax collector. W. D. walked inside and surveyed the interior. The cash register was plainly in view in the middle of a long counter on the left. Nell Brown, tall and thin, wearing a long butcher's apron, watched as the young man scanned the building. He abruptly left without a purchase.

W. D. apprised Buck of the situation. This looked like an easy mark. Nervous and apprehensive without Clyde along, W. D. didn't want to be put in a threatening position. The woman behind the counter looked harmless enough. Buck drove the car one block further north, then turned behind the school onto Mt. Nord Street. Buck waited in the car. The weather was quite warm, and W. D. unbuttoned the top buttons of his white shirt. Mrs. Brown looked out towards the school ground and noticed the young man returning, walking across the schoolyard. His white shirt unbuttoned at the collar, and wearing a "tomato-pie" golf hat, Mrs. Brown

The Brown Grocery, Lafayette Street, Fayetteville, Arkansas. Originally one story, the second story was added as an apartment by the Browns to meet the University of Arkansas student demand following World War II. (Photo courtesy of Phillip Steele)

thought he looked quite handsome and dapper. W. D. crossed the street and entered the store. This time he strode purposefully towards the counter. Mrs. Brown glanced around and realized that the store was empty of customers. Aside from the stranger, the only other person in the building was the hired hand, Ewell Trammell, busy up front sorting apples into the window bins. The stranger called for Trammell to come near. Mrs. Brown, sensing trouble, walked to the register and shut the drawer. This caught the attention of W. D., who immediately pulled a Colt Government model .45 automatic pistol from his coat pocket. W. D. ordered the pair to not make a move or a sound or he would kill them. He began to tug at the register drawer, but he could not open it. He turned to glare at Mrs. Brown, and his cold stare convinced her that there was no use in resisting. She depressed the drawer release with her thumb, hiding her fingers from view, then immediately put her hands back into her apron pockets. W. D. scooped out the money and stuffed his pockets. His nervousness was revealed, as Mrs. Brown later recounted that he visibly shook as he ransacked the register. Coins spilled onto the floor, and he bent and carefully searched them all out. Then he turned on the hired hand and frisked him. He took a quarter, a nickel, and five pennies from Ewell Trammell. The total take of the robbery was between $17.00 and $20.00.

Mrs. Brown had recently inherited two magnificent diamond rings from a friend, Mrs. Puckett, upon her death. Mrs. Puckett's husband had been a Fayetteville jeweler and had carefully crafted the rings from very high quality jewels for his wife. Mrs. Brown was careful to conceal the rings from W. D. Jones during the robbery, and he walked out of the store unaware that he had overlooked the only items of significant value in the store. Before he left the store, W. D. demanded the keys to the Model A delivery truck parked outside. Nell Brown told W. D. that the keys had been left in the ignition of the vehicle. What she didn't tell him was the car's battery was dead and the crank was missing. Anxious to get away, Jones flung open the front door and ran outside towards the vehicle. At the moment he was barreling through the doorway, seven-year-old Wanda Audit was standing on the steps outside reaching for the door handle. She was pushed away and knocked down by the force of his exit as W. D. bolted for the delivery truck.

The vehicle would not start. Undeterred, Jones opened the door and pushed the Model A down the hill. He hopped in, engaged the clutch, and the motor caught. He drove around the block to Mt. Nord, then abandoned the delivery truck, letting it roll downhill and crash into a tree.

It is interesting to note that little Wanda Audit was able to contribute to this particular chapter in the life of Bonnie and Clyde personally, as Mrs. Wanda Audit Montgomery is still alive at the time of this writing. In letters and telephone interviews, Wanda related that, at the time of the robbery, she lived beside Brown's Grocery, at 113 Lafayette. Wanda states that she was going to the store to purchase a loaf of bread when she was knocked to the ground by the fleeing bandit. At the time, it was believed that the outlaw was Clyde Barrow.

Mrs. Audit told of being picked up and comforted by Mrs. Nell Brown and her mother as she lay crying. She pointed to the fleeing outlaw and stated, "That man knocked me down." Mrs. Brown stated, "That man was Clyde Barrow." When asked why Mrs. Brown thought he was Clyde, Wanda stated that posters affixed to store windows and posted in the post office resembled the man, and it was known from radio broadcasts that the Barrows were active in the area, having been involved in the shootout at Neosho, Missouri, a few weeks beforehand.

In the days afterwards, Nell Brown was asked several times to identify the man through police posters and pictures. She would pick out Clyde Barrow's picture as "possibly" being the person in the store. Wanda Audit recalled that her uncle, who lived on Mt. Nord Street, watched as a Ford car occupied by a man and woman awaited a third person, who ran to the car, which then sped away. It is possible this third person could have been Blanche Barrow, but this part of the story has never been substantiated. We have only Wanda Montgomery's uncle mentioning a man and *woman* waiting.

Mr. Bates had noticed the suspicious vehicle and the young man walking from store to store, and he called in the vehicle's license number. The deputies began to search the area for the car. Because Brown's Grocery was equipped with a telephone, it is believed that Nell Brown herself called in the robbery shortly after it occurred. Sheriff Harley Gover was out of town at the time helping investigate criminal activity in Missouri.

The group fled south, out of Fayetteville towards the town of Alma. Deputies were in pursuit, but the powerful Ford pulled away and was soon out of sight. The Fayetteville police station radioed ahead to Alma's Marshall Humphreys, giving him a description of the car and the license number.

In the meantime, the fleeing robbers had started looking for another vehicle, perhaps reasoning that the police must have seen the vehicle or obtained the license number to have reacted so quickly after the robbery. They stopped at the town of Winslow and spotted a likely vehicle at the home of Mr. and Mrs. John Rogers. Mrs. Rogers was alone at the time, her husband having gone to help out a neighbor. Mr. Rogers apparently had taken the car keys with him, as Mrs. Rogers could not—or would not—produce the keys to the automobile. She was threatened with her life and suffered a severe beating with a heavy chain. The bandits pushed the automobile out of the garage and over the hill towards a bluff drop-off, then drove off in their original automobile.

In terrible pain from the beating, Mrs. Rogers arose from where she lay on the ground and chased down the car, steering it into a tree to stop it. A local physician treated Mrs. Rogers for her injuries, but her wounds were of such severity that she was transported to the Fort Smith hospital and remained in critical condition for several days.

It has been debated if this incident actually involved the Barrows. The Barrow family always denied it, but it has been documented that police investigating the crime showed pictures of various criminals to Mrs. Rogers, and she identified one of the men who assaulted her as Buck Barrow. Although this was not an action typical of the Barrow gang, it must be noted that, during the Fayetteville robbery and subsequent flight back to Fort Smith, there is evidence that Clyde, generally a calming force amongst the group, was not present. W. D. Jones was very excitable and often acted impulsively, putting the group at risk on several occasions because of his rash behavior.

The group proceeded to Alma. Marshall Humphreys was without a vehicle at the time, so he called his friend, A. M. ("Red") Salyers, for assistance. Mr. Salyers, a former deputy, accompanied the Marshall to a vantage point on the northern edge of Alma. The pair parked to watch the road when Weber Wilson, a local auto mechanic, drove up and engaged them in conversation. As they talked, an automobile topped the hill at a high rate of speed. At the sound of the approaching car, Marshall Humphreys called out to Weber Wilson to get off the road, and Salyers pulled their vehicle forward and out of the way, but the oncoming vehicle crashed into Weber Wilson's car. Though shaken by the collision, Wilson was very upset at the damage done to his new auto, a light blue Chevrolet two-door coupe. He proceeded to pick up two large rocks with the intention of attacking those responsible for the damage to his vehicle. As he approached the other vehicle, he was met with the barrel of a gun. Weber dropped the rocks and fled to a nearby canebrake.

At this time, Humphreys and Salyers left their vehicle and walked back to the wreck. Humphreys noticed the vehicle license number as being that of the vehicle involved in the Fayetteville robbery, and they approached the vehicle with drawn guns. Marshall Humphreys, a portly, mild mannered man with very little experience in law enforcement, carried a .38 revolver. Salyers' weapon was a Winchester lever action 30-30, which he had recently taken in payment of a debt.

Marshall Humphreys of Alma, Arkansas, was killed during a road block attempt on U.S. Highway 71, north of Alma. (Photo courtesy of Dallas Historical Library)

The doors to the wrecked Ford swung open, each of the occupants resting weapons in the window frames.

The bandits opened fire, and Marshall Humphreys was hit immediately. He fell mortally wounded, apparently from a shotgun blast administered by Buck Barrow. Buck's shotgun jammed, and W. D. Jones, wielding a Browning Automatic Rifle, fired at Red Salyers. But Jones was not the accomplished master of the heavy machine gun that Clyde Barrow was, and Salyers was able to avoid being hit by running and dodging. Salyers kept his head and returned fire at the pair, emptying his Winchester. There was a lull in the shooting as W. D. reloaded the BAR. This gave Salyers the chance to take more substantial cover, so he ran behind a nearby farmhouse. By this time, W. D. had reloaded the BAR and began to fire once again in Salyers' direction. The metal-jacketed bullets penetrated the farmhouse and kicked up dust around a nearby family picking strawberries on a hillside behind the farmhouse. Salyers was able to reach the protection of a rock chimney and there reloaded his rifle.

W. D. had once again emptied the BAR, and the outlaws turned their attentions to leaving the scene. They finally commandeered Salyers' car and made good their escape, but not before Red Salyers got off more shots, at least one of which struck a tire on the car.

Officers who later searched the Barrow vehicle found 40 empty shells from the BAR scattered around it. The interior of the car contained 500 machine gun cartridges and various firearms, along with vehicle license plates from five different states.

Shortly after the shooting, six-year-old Gayle Kaundark, whose home overlooked the scene of the wreck, walked down to the road and approached Marshall Humphreys, who lay bleeding at the roadside. Humphreys asked for a drink of water, and the youngster ran home to fulfill the wishes of the wounded peace officer. Marshal Humphreys died shortly afterwards in a Fort Smith hospital, but not before he was able to identify Buck from police photos.

A local citizen, B. C. Ames, reported seeing the Barrows escaping in Salyers' car and being fired at as they raced by him. The bandits' trail was lost until their car was found eight miles east of Van Buren, Arkansas, a few hours later. They had obviously changed cars again to throw the lawmen off their trail.

Knowing that the authorities would probably quickly discover the Dennis Tourist Court retreat, W. D. and Buck drove directly to the courts and shared the events of their fateful trip with their friends. Clyde instructed W. D. and Buck to stay at the courts to finish gathering all of their possessions while he took the women and searched out a new and safer location. The women were nearly hysterical from stress and fear of being found at any moment.

Clyde drove north into the mountains and finally found a solitary spot where he could leave the women. Although extremely tired from the day's events, he returned to Fort Smith to pick up his brother and W. D. and return them to the new, but temporary, hideout.

According to various reports, the Barrows passed through Fayetteville one other time on April 9 or 10. A Fayetteville citizen, Merle Cruse, reported his car license, 15-368 Arkansas 1934, stolen about this time—the same plate that later showed up on the car that Bonnie and Clyde were driving when killed in northeast Louisiana.

Clyde, at some point, decided that Billie Parker was no longer needed to help with Bonnie, so he told her she needed to return to Dallas. There were simply too many in the group now for the size of their coupe, and food and medical supplies were always scarce. Billie protested Clyde's decision, but to no avail. W. D. drove the party to Enid, Oklahoma, on the evening of June 24, 1933. They spotted a dark sedan, and soon they were fleeing south in the newly-stolen vehicle. The sedan turned out to be a doctor's car that had some badly needed medical supplies in the trunk.

The Barrows drove past Oklahoma City late on Sunday night, June 26, 1933. Clyde had again changed the license plate. They arrived at the Sherman, Texas, railroad depot on the morning of June 27, and Clyde gave train fare to Billie. This was another highly emotional parting for the sisters. Billie later reported that while she stood watching Clyde's car pull away from the depot that morning, she strongly felt she would never see her beloved sister Bonnie again.

⚜15⚜

ON THE ROAD AGAIN

The Barrow Gang was back on the road again in Oklahoma, often leaving the main roads to avoid any possible problems with the authorities. Their ammunition was extremely low, until they successfully robbed the National Guard Armory in Enid, Oklahoma, on July 7. Well aware that this was a federal crime, Clyde was even more skeptical about renting a cabin, so they traveled at night and slept in the woods when secluded spots could be found. They traveled through Oklahoma for several weeks before entering Summer County, Kansas, turning northwest to avoid the large city of Wichita.

It had been a long time between baths, and rest on a good mattress seemed like a good idea. Clyde decided to stop near Great Bend, Kansas, shortly before sunset on the evening of June 29, 1933, and they rented two cabins. They had sufficient funds for a few days' rent and Bonnie's medical needs, but Clyde knew the need for additional funds would soon become critical. He didn't feel that he could leave Bonnie, so he told Buck and W. D. that he expected them to do the necessary robbing until Bonnie's burns improved. Over the next several weeks, Buck and W. D. committed several robberies, usually of small stores or gasoline stations, throughout Kansas. They kept their robberies away from their Great Bend headquarters and from the southeastern part of the state near Joplin, Missouri.

As robbing became easier and more routine for the men, and as Bonnie's wounds improved, the gang became more openly aggressive. On the morning of July 18, 1933, for example, Clyde, Buck, W. D., Bonnie, and Blanche drove up to a Fort Dodge, Kansas, service station and took all of the station's cash. The job was so easy, the apparently arrogant Barrow Gang then robbed two more stations in Fort Dodge before leaving town.

Using Clyde's uncanny ability to avoid roadblocks, they left Kansas and drove into Missouri before the day was over. Around 10:00 P.M. the gang arrived at the Red Crown Tourist Camp, a few miles south of Platte City, Missouri. The desk clerk registered the party into two cabins. When the attractive lady who registered for the group paid for the cabins in coins, the clerk thought it was strange, so he looked at the car more closely when the new tenant went to rejoin her party. Seeing that one of the women was bandaged quite heavily, the clerk became even more suspicious. After everyone was settled into the two cabins, Blanche returned to the office and gas station to buy five sandwiches and five beers.

The next morning, the clerk saw that their car had been carefully hidden in the carport and the drawn curtains had never been opened. The three men in the party had not been seen in the open. This unusual behavior added to the clerk's apprehension, and he wondered if perhaps these guests were involved in something illegal. He finally felt so strongly about these secretive guests that he decided to tell his employer, H. D. Hauser, who telephoned Captain William Baxter with the Missouri Highway Patrol.

When Captain Baxter learned that one of the females in the group was heavily bandaged, he believed these people just might be the slippery Barrow Gang. He contacted his friend, Holt Coffey, Sheriff of Platte County, and instructed him to wait for his arrival from Kansas City. Baxter and

Coffey carefully laid out the plans they felt would best handle the situation. The Platte City Police Department sent two officers, Sergeant Thomas Witherspoon and Officer L. A. Ellis, to meet the sheriff. Deputies George Borden, George Highfill, and Lincoln Baker, along with Constables Byron Fisher and Thomas Hullet, also encircled the tourist court.

The Barrow Gang needed this time off the road to rest and recuperate. The medical supplies found in the doctor's car had helped, but they were minimal when it came to Bonnie's needs. They ate sandwiches purchased from the Red Crown Station and tourist court office and slept on beds and chairs. Clyde was nervous about driving, since their only car was the one stolen in nearby Kansas, so he started walking along the highway toward Platte City, where he hoped to find a pharmacy where he could get the supplies needed for all their wounded. He finally began hitchhiking and was soon picked up. He was back by 8:00 P.M. with the medical supplies, and the group tended to their wounded. Totally unaware of the posse slowly and quietly forming around their cabins, most of them were asleep by 10:00 P.M.

Because of the numerous unsuccessful attempts to capture the Barrow Gang over the preceding months, Sheriff Coffey and Captain Baxter made arrangements for a local armored car to be filled with several officers and positioned to block the Barrow's car in the carport. Spotlights from other officers' cars were then all aimed at the cabin doors as Sheriff Coffey stepped up and banged loudly on the cabin door as he yelled out, "This is the police; open up!"

Blanche, the only one awake, shouted back, "You'll have to wait until I get dressed." Clyde, W. D., and Buck were all awakened by Blanche's shouting and began grabbing their weapons.

Pounding a second time, Coffey shouted, "I need to talk to your men folk!"

Clyde picked Bonnie up from a bed and ran with W. D. through the carport door. Just as Clyde threw Bonnie into their car, W. D. screamed out, "Our car's blocked by an armored car."

Clyde grabbed one of the Browning Automatic Rifles taken from the Enid Armory and began spraying bullets at the armored car and toward the police car spotlights. At such close range, even the armored car was penetrated, wounding several officers inside. Buck was also spraying the lawmen, and Deputy Highfill realized they must pull the armored car away because it could not take the intensity of the firepower being rained on it.

As the armored car was backed away slowly, a bullet struck the horn on one of the police cars, causing it to stick. Many in the posse took this to be a signal to stop shooting, so they did. The three bandits took major advantage of the lull in the shooting by increasing their attack on the lawmen.

During the fracas, Buck was rendered unconscious by two bullets to the head. Blanche somehow half dragged Buck to the car, got in beside him, and, while Clyde was starting the car, W. D. continued shooting to cover them as they sped away, dodging the police cars at seventy miles an hour. They first headed north, then took a dirt road to the east. The car was full of screaming, half-conscious passengers, and Clyde was searching for a place to stop and look after their wounds. After that was accomplished, Clyde drove as fast as the Ford would travel throughout the night.

Other than Buck's head wounds, that were bleeding profusely, bullets had shattered the car's windshield as they crashed out of the tourist court. The flying glass wounded Blanche badly and entered her left eye. As blood poured from Blanche's face, she screamed out, "Stop! Stop! I can't see. They have blinded me!" Thereafter, numerous surgeons tried through the years to save Blanche's eye, but they were not successful.

The lawmen at the site assessed their wounded and alerted authorities throughout the Midwest to be on the lookout for the badly injured Barrow Gang. Deputy George Highfill was seriously wounded in the knee when gunfire from the

BLANCH
BARROW
AFTER BEING
FINGERPRINTED
July 24th 1933

Blanche Barrow shortly after left eye was badly injured from glass during shootout with Iowa Policeman, July 24, 1933. (Photo courtesy of Marie Barrow Scoma)

Barrows' automatic weapons penetrated the armored car. He was treated at St. Joseph Hospital in Kansas City, Missouri. Sheriff Coffey received a neck wound, and his son, a simple bystander at the shooting, was severely wounded in the arm. He and his father were both treated at Kansas City's Bethany Hospital. Almost all of the officers received at least minor wounds.

Around dusk the following evening, Clyde found a wooded spot between Dexter and Redfield, Iowa, called Dexfield Park, about twenty-five miles from Des Moines. This heavily wooded, twenty-acre park had a branch of the Middle Raccoon River running through it. Finding a small clearing, Clyde and W. D. managed to get all the wounded out of the car and laid them on pallets constructed from newspapers and blankets. After washing their wounds and applying alcohol, salve, and other medicines, Clyde felt Buck had recovered sufficiently to be left in charge. He and W. D. drove into the hamlet of Perry, Iowa, approximately eighteen miles northwest of their new hideout, where they got food and more supplies, then stole a car belonging to Edward Stoner.

Upon their return to the hideout, Clyde put Bonnie into the car and drove through the park, making note of all escape routes in case they were cornered again. While on this scouting trip, Clyde noted a large bag of used bandages in the car and knew the bag could be detrimental if found, so he stopped the car and set the bag on fire.

Homer Penn, a local farmer, found the bag of partially burned bandages as he was walking through the park several hours later. Recalling the news on the radio about Texas outlaws possibly being in the region, Penn called Sheriff C. A. Knee in Adel, the county seat. Knee called a special deputy he used when needed, John Love. The two began planning how the Barrows might be trapped. They first sent out two deputies to survey the park, and the two soon located the two autos and wounded bandits. One kept watch over the area from a hiding place in the brush while the other hurried to a telephone from which Sheriff Knee was informed.

After everyone had been fed, treated, and had slept and cleaned themselves, Clyde began to carefully consider their options. It was late in the day on Monday, July 23, 1933. He carefully noted how badly his brother Buck now looked. He had watched several others die during his brief lifetime, and Buck's appearance reminded him of those people. He feared Buck might be near death. Clyde also recalled the promise that he and Buck had made to their mother—should either ever be close to death, they would be brought home to die.

Clyde Barrow cleaning and oiling his guns with Bonnie Parker at campsite. (Photo courtesy of Marie Barrow Scoma)

Clyde decided that, although Dexfield Park was serving them well, his sixth sense was telling him it was time to leave.

Clyde and W. D. started making plans to leave for Texas the next morning. Officers Knee and Love were also making plans and forming a dependable posse of capable men to use in capturing, once and for all, the notorious Barrow Gang. Iowa Governor Clyde P. Herring was even contacted about the possibility of calling out a National Guard unit to surround the park if needed. Sheriff Knee had brought together the largest body of men to ever gather as an outlaw posse. Forty National Guardsmen, all of the local officers, and a hundred or more farmers with their squirrel rifles had all met and received their assignments for bringing the Barrow Gang to an end at sunrise the next morning.

As the Barrows were awaking, W. D. started a fire and began roasting breakfast wieners. Sheriff Knee signaled his forces to move in. Bonnie was the first to see the posse and screamed, "Clyde, it's the law!" Clyde ran to the car where all their arms were stored. He tossed a Browning Automatic Rifle to W. D. and picked up one for himself, and the two opened fire on the approaching posse. Bonnie dragged herself to the car and crawled into the back seat. Blanche helped Buck crawl to the car. Firing continually as he ran toward the car, Clyde jumped in, started the car, and drove a few yards before bullets from a posse man's rifle shattered his left arm. Clyde lost control of the car and crashed into a tree stump. Clyde and W. D. jumped out and tried to free the car bumper from the stump, but it couldn't be moved. Clyde ordered everyone out and into the Stoner car nearby. While this was happening, W. D. was struck several times in the face with shotgun pellets.

As the deadly automatic rifle fire subsided, while the Barrows were running to the second car, Knee's posse closed in tighter. Their gunfire shattered car windows, flattened tires, and even punctured the car's gas tank before the outlaws could move. Noting the uselessness of the car, Clyde ordered his associates out of the Stoner car and into the brush for survival. Buck Barrow was assisted out of the car by Blanche; however, several more bullets hit him in the chest and back, causing him to collapse before he reached the safety of the nearby thicket. The hysterical Blanche, screaming for Clyde and W. D. to come to Buck's rescue, threw herself over Buck's body in an attempt to shield her husband from the continual onslaught of bullets coming from the Iowa posse.

As he leaped from the car, Clyde was shot in the leg as he tried to get to Buck. Dragging them into the brush with his good arm, Clyde told them to sit tight while he left to find another car and return for them.

"Take Blanche with you. Don't leave her here to die," Buck shouted to Clyde as he ran.

"No, Daddy, I'm not leaving you!" Blanche cried out.

Clyde left W. D. to look after Bonnie and Buck, and he limped toward the river where he hoped to cross and find a vehicle. As the rain of bullets subsided, Blanche screamed, "Hold your fire. He's dying. Please don't shoot anymore."

W. D. continued to help Bonnie toward the river. Suddenly, they heard a barrage of gunfire from the direction in which Clyde had run, and they assumed that their friend and lover had finally been brought down. Both simply lay down in the grass and cried profusely while holding each other tightly. Their anguish was soon relieved, though, when they looked up to see none other than Clyde Barrow coming through the woods to assist them. Clyde led Bonnie and W. D. toward the river where they were continually fired upon as they attempted to cross, but as astonishing as it seems, they reached the other side, where Clyde had his companions lay down in a cornfield. He set out again to look for some form of transportation to get them all out of there.

At a nearby house, Clyde found four men—Valley Fellers, Valley's son, and Marvin and Walter Spillars. Fellers pulled a long chain of keys from his overalls when Clyde threatened all their lives with his .45 pistol. He whistled for Bonnie and W. D., and they half crawled toward the farmhouse, where Clyde helped them into the car once he got it started.

Blanche pleaded with the posse to get Buck a doctor. Even though one came right away, he could do little for the dying Buck Barrow. Blanche fought to stay with her husband, but the posse men pulled her away. Officers then quickly drove Buck and Blanche to King's Daughters Hospital in Perry, Iowa. As soon as the news reached Buck's family, Mrs. Barrow, daughter Nell, and brother L. C. left Dallas and drove toward Perry, Iowa.

After Clyde washed W. D. Jones' wounds so he could drive, he passed out from loss of blood. W. D. drove the three to Polk City, Iowa, where they stole a better car and continued traveling west toward Denver. As they drove into Colorado City, they took a newspaper from a mailbox, and they were all shocked, especially Bonnie, to see an article telling that Bonnie Parker, with several wounds, was being hidden away by authorities in a Denver hospital.

"We can't go there," Clyde moaned. "With such ridiculous folklore, they'll be looking for us all over Denver."

They found a wooded area in which to once again rest and they stayed there several days, contemplating what their futures might be. Clyde and Bonnie's wounds gradually healed, and Clyde was finally able to take over the driving again. At this time, W. D. Jones must have decided he had no future with his friends Bonnie and Clyde, so he bought a bus ticket to Houston and left.

Buck died in the Perry, Iowa, hospital on July 29, 1933, only a short time after his family arrived from Texas. A. M. Salyers, who had witnessed the killing of his good friend Marshall Humphreys in Alma, Arkansas, also arrived in time to interview Buck. Asked if he recognized him, Buck told Salyers, "Yeah, I know you. Me and W. D. shot at you over in Arkansas one time before you ran into the barn." Buck was careful not to mention Clyde's name during his deathbed interview.

Lawmen and Texas newsmen all helped with the arrangements to return Buck's remains to Texas and plan for a proper funeral service at the Sparkman-Holtz-Brand Funeral Home. Reverend Frank P. Dailey, of the Cedar Valley Baptist Church, led the service. Some fifty mourners attended, including Buck's first wife, Elizabeth Quick, and her son, Marvin Ivan Barrow, Jr. Numerous lawmen and newsmen were also in attendance, just in case the rumor of Buck's notorious brother, Clyde Barrow, finding a way to attend the services was more than a rumor.

After the ceremony, a rumor did spread that Clyde attended wearing women's clothing. This author asked Marie Barrow about this point and was told, "I wouldn't have put it past Clyde pulling a prank such as that, but if he was there he certainly would have at least spoken to his mother and other family members."

Buck's remains were interred at the Western Heights Cemetery in West Dallas.

Without his cherished brother Buck, and friends W. D. Jones and Raymond Hamilton for support, Clyde was somewhat at a loss as to where to turn. During the weeks that followed, almost every crime of any kind around the Southwest was being blamed on Bonnie and Clyde, when in reality the couple was not responsible for any of them. Such false accusations greatly upset Bonnie and Clyde as they continued to travel back roads, camp in wooded areas, and depend on what few relatives and friends they had whom they could trust. Dallas authorities concluded it would be only a short time until the infamous Bonnie and Clyde would be brought down.

⊰16⊱

THE U.S. GOVERNMENT GETS INVOLVED

Authorities continued to maintain surveillance of the Barrow and Parker homes. They had formed a posse, and planned to ambush the couple in the event such an opportunity arose. Clyde's mother was to have a birthday on November 1, 1933, and it had become commonplace for both the Barrow and Parker families to gather for food, cake, and fellowship at a rural location in West Dallas County.

Fearing lawmen might have learned of their meeting, the families kept the picnic short. Since no lawmen appeared at the brief family encounter, the group decided to meet once again the next evening at the same location and stay longer. This proved to be a mistake. A farmer who had witnessed the frolicking group picnicking in a most unusual location reported to authorities seeing them at the same spot the next day. Excited by the prospect of bringing down Bonnie and Clyde at one of their family meetings, the posse, directed by Sheriff Smoot Schmit, moved in to quietly surround the family party.

Clyde felt uneasy about the quietness as he drove slowly to the location where family members were waiting. The nervous posse opened fire on Clyde's auto before they should have, and Clyde turned and raced out of the area as hundreds of bullets riddled the car.

Clyde blocked the road where Thomas James and Paul Reich were returning from a Scottish Rite function. Naturally, the men at first objected to giving up their Model B Ford sedan, but after Clyde suddenly shattered a window with a shotgun blast, they turned over their vehicle with no further hesitation. The flying glass did injure the men, who were picked up a few minutes later by another member returning from the same Scottish Rite meeting, and they were taken to a Grand Prairie doctor for treatment.

The next morning, Sheriff Schmit and one of his deputies, Ed Castor, studied the Ford car Clyde had abandoned after the unsuccessful ambush. Some of the officers had been armed with Thompson submachine guns, which fired the short .45 automatic pistol cartridge. It was evident, from the numerous dents on the exterior of the car, that the Thompson gun lacked the power to penetrate the heavy-bodied new Fords. The officers decided that a weapon with more power was needed because they were tired of being "outrun and outgunned."

Deputy Ted Hinton knew that Clyde Barrow favored the big Browning Automatic Rifle, so Hinton surmised that officers would need to be similarly armed. Schmit and Hinton requested permission to borrow the automatic weapons from the Texas National Guard. Captain Weldon Dowis was the Commander of Texas National Guard Company E, 144th Infantry, 36th Division, at the time Schmit and Hinton made the request for the Browning Automatic Rifles. Since the rifles were government property, Dowis refused the request. Deputy Hinton then contacted his friend, U.S. Congressman Hatton Summers, for assistance. Soon afterward, Captain Dowis received a letter from Congressman Summers requesting the two weapons be loaned to the lawmen. The Congressman further stated he would take full responsibility for the transaction.

⊰17⊱

HENRY METHVIN
JOINS THE GANG

Raymond Hamilton negotiated with James Mullin, a cell-mate who was to be released before Hamilton, to pay him $1,000.00 to help Hamilton escape after Mullin was released. Raymond Hamilton wanted Mullin to seek help from Bonnie and Clyde. When Mullin was released, he went to Dallas, where he found Floyd Hamilton, Raymond's brother, who soon contacted Clyde.

On January 14, 1934, Floyd visited his brother at the prison to discuss final details. The next day, Floyd Hamilton and James Mullin hid two automatic pistols near the wood cutting area on the prison farm. Later that day, Trustee Yost retrieved the hidden weapons, smuggled them into the prison barracks, and delivered one to Raymond Hamilton and one to Joe Palmer, another friend, who was serving a twenty-five-year term for kidnapping a child.

The next day, the two reported to the wood cutting area as directed. It was a very foggy morning; visibility was limited. Bonnie and Clyde drove to an area near the place where the two inmates were to be cutting wood and waited. They had earlier picked up Mullin, who guided Clyde to the planned meeting place. Clyde brought out his favorite Browning Automatic Rifle and gave Mullin a .45 automatic pistol before they stepped out and walked a few yards toward the wood cutting site to wait for their friends.

Bonnie, who remained in the car composing another poem, had been instructed to begin honking the horn on their Ford when the firing began so Raymond and the others could better find the vehicle in the fog.

Another inmate friend of Hamilton's, Henry Methvin, from northwest Louisiana, had agreed to join the escapees. His assignment was to take guns from the guards when the drop was made on them by the party. As the woodcutting party reached their assigned location, the guards challenged Hamilton and a few of the others as to why they were in that particular place. Palmer and Hamilton pulled their guns to fire. Clyde and Mullin fired over the heads of the guards as Hamilton commanded the guards to drop their weapons and ordered Methvin to pick them up. Bonnie had the car started and was leaning on the car horn as soon as the first shots were heard.

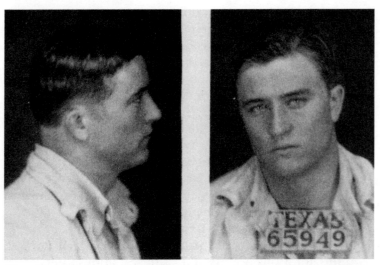

Henry Methvin rode with the Barrow Gang and turned in his friends, Bonnie Parker and Clyde Barrow. (Photo courtesy of Dallas Public Library—Texas Prison photo)

As Methvin followed Hamilton, the others also followed. W. H. Bybee came along. He was serving a life term. J. B. French, who had been sentenced to twelve years, also followed, as the area exploded with chaotic gunfire from all directions. Clyde and Mullin were the first to reach the car, followed by fellow inmates who hoped to find room for themselves in the vehicle. Clyde quickly took over the situation by ordering four of the men—Palmer, Methvin, French, and Bybee—to crowd into the car's trunk. Mullin then moved into the right passenger seat next to Bonnie. Clyde drove while Hamilton sat on Mullin's lap.

The outlaws sped northwest, following backcountry roads to Dallas. Clyde stopped their car a few miles after starting, opened the trunk, and, explaining the danger of so many together, divided the party. French and Bybee were now on their own, while Methvin, Hamilton, and Palmer continued on with Bonnie and Clyde, hoping for yet a better day and a new life.

Realizing that probably every lawman in Texas would soon learn of the escape and Bonnie and Clyde's participation in it, Clyde decided going north would be foolish. He immediately turned and headed toward Houston, but they only stayed forty-eight hours before once again heading back toward Dallas. Hamilton remembered he owed Mullin the $1,000 he promised for his help in the escape, so he made plans to rob the bank in Lancaster, Texas, only a short distance south of Dallas so he could pay his debt.

Director of Texas Prisons, Lee Simmons, had learned that Bonnie and Clyde, without any question whatsoever, had been involved in the Texas escape planned out by Raymond Hamilton. Simmons, like so many others, was determined to somehow bring down the couple.

Receiving permission from Texas Governor Miriam Ferguson to proceed with plans to form a special force to stop the notorious Bonnie and Clyde, Simmons interviewed several qualified lawmen before choosing the former Texas Ranger Frank Hamer. By his own admission, Frank Hamer had been involved in over 50 shootouts in a career spanning three decades. At 6'3" and 232 pounds, Hamer was an imposing figure. His face and body were pockmarked with the scars from 23 different gunshot wounds. Simmons knew that Hamer possessed the one trait that most law officers who challenged Clyde Barrow could not muster—the man was absolutely fearless, and he would oftentimes expose himself to gunfire in order to locate his adversary. Hamer was blessed with extraordinary vision and was an incredible shot with his Remington Model 8 repeating rifle.

"Ma'am, I want to take Bonnie and Clyde off the road," was Simmons' explanation for choosing Hamer, who was a political enemy of Governor Ferguson.

On February 1, 1934, Simmons drove up to the governor's mansion in Austin to discuss this with Governor Ferguson. The Governor soon agreed with Simmons' choice. "We don't hold a grudge against Hamer and feel he is the best man for the job. Whatever it takes to get these killers off the streets."

Simmons drove from the governor's mansion directly to Frank Hamer's home, where he related his conversation with the Governor, and pleaded with Hamer to come back to work for the State of Texas. He would act as a special agent commissioned to put together a force to bring down the notorious Bonnie and Clyde and the rest of the Barrow Gang as soon as possible.

Hamer explained to Simmons, "Lee, I make $500.00 a month as a security consultant with an oil company now."

"Frank, you know we can't match that, but money is not your number one priority. About $180.00 a month, plus the satisfaction of stopping these folks, is the best we can do."

Lee then assured Hamer that the project would be entirely under his control and he would be backed up to the limit. After deliberation over a cigarette or two, Hamer finally said, "Okay, Lee. I'll take the job."

Meanwhile, Bonnie and Clyde had found their way back to Dallas, and a reunion with several of their gangster friends to plan their future direction was held sometime around February 19, 1934. When the reunion was over, Bonnie and Clyde drifted back home, while some of their gangster friends proceeded to Ranger, Texas, and burglarized a National Guard Armory. Later that day, Floyd Hamilton met the gangsters at a pre-planned location between Lancaster, Texas, and Dallas, where Hamilton took the weapons to hide for use in their next bank robbery. Plans were made to meet again one week later near Cedar Hill and rob the Lancaster Bank.

After selecting several fresh automobiles to use in their upcoming robberies and working out details at an abandoned farmhouse in Grand Prairie, on Tuesday, February 27, the robbing began. Clyde, Raymond Hamilton, and Henry Methvin loaded all their weapons in the one car Clyde was driving and drove southwest toward Lancaster. Clyde parked next to the R. P. Henry and Son Bank when they arrived in Lancaster. Leaving Methvin as their lookout, Clyde and Raymond walked toward the bank's entrance with their weapons carefully concealed under their coats. One of the bank owners, L. L. Henry, stood behind the teller's window serving a customer, Olin Worley, as the two entered the lobby.

"Open the safe! Do as we say and you'll live through this," Clyde shouted as he pointed his sawed off shotgun toward Mr. Henry.

Raymond pressed his pistol into the back of Olin Worley and ordered him to drop to the floor. As Worley began to slide down, Raymond noticed the man had some $300.00 in cash in his hand, which Hamilton quickly took.

As Mr. Henry got the safe open, Clyde carefully watched the front and Worley while Raymond grabbed up all the cash he could see in the vault. As the bandits rushed out to their car, Banker Henry calmly walked to his telephone and called Sheriff John Ciesa. The robbery only took a few minutes, then all was calm. Not a shot was fired.

As Worley and Henry attempted to describe the robbers, the Sheriff quickly determined that the pair must have been

Raymond Hamilton and Clyde Barrow. When Henry totaled the bank's losses, they amounted to $4,138.20.

The gang drove to where their girlfriends were waiting on a farm a few miles north, picked up different cars, and hurried away. Clyde, Bonnie, and Henry Methvin were in the front seat of their car, and the others were in the back. Clyde glanced into the car's rearview mirror, and was shocked to see Hamilton taking some of the bank loot and stuffing it into his shirt before they had a chance to stop and divide up the money.

They drove on into Indiana, with Clyde carefully avoiding the dozens of roadblocks that were set up for several days following the Lancaster robbery. Hamilton's attempt to take money without Clyde knowing and conflicts between Bonnie and Hamilton's girlfriend, Mary O'Dare, also riding with the gang, caused the group to break up. This was the last "business transaction" Clyde had with Raymond Hamilton. After leaving Hamilton and his girlfriend in Indiana, Clyde stole another car and turned back toward Dallas with Bonnie and Methvin.

Authorities soon learned of the gang's alleged split, but became confused when they learned that Raymond Hamilton and Mary O'Dare had also returned to the Dallas area. On Saturday, March 31, 1934, Raymond drove up to a bank in the tiny community of West, Texas, and left Mary with the car while he ran into the bank and took $1,200.00. While racing away from the bank to the south, the car slid on a muddy road into a ditch. Raymond flagged down a passing car driven by Mrs. Cameron Gunter, with her young son, and forced them to drive him and Mary to Houston, where Raymond freed the lady and her son.

After an Easter holiday family gathering in April of 1934, a black V-8 sedan carrying Bonnie, Clyde, and Henry Methvin was moving east along Texas Highway 114 before turning north on Dove Lane. William Schieffer, a local farmer, happened to see the car pull off the road, park, and the occupants begin napping. Actually, it was Bonnie and Clyde who napped while Methvin served as their lookout.

Speeding had become a major problem on that road, and three new motorcycle officers had recently been assigned to cruise that stretch of Highway 114. Patrolmen E. B. Wheeler, H. D. Murphy, and Polk Ivy had been patrolling since noon that day and had all seen the black sedan. Two of the patrolmen stopped to rest and check their bikes on the other side of the road.

As they started up their bikes again, with apparently no concern for the parked sedan nearby, Bonnie awoke and, shaking Clyde, she whispered, "Wake up Clyde. It's the law."

Clyde immediately saw that the patrolmen meant no harm as one leisurely parked his bike and slowly walked toward the car. Methvin, however, had only ridden with Bonnie and Clyde for a short time, and was not fully familiar with how they operated. Kidnapping lawmen, for instance, was what Clyde meant when he said, "Let's take them!" Methvin misunderstood Clyde's comment and opened fire on the patrolmen.

Personnel from the Foust Funeral Home in Grapevine were the first to arrive after the shooting, and they reported finding Wheeler dead at the scene and Murphy only barely alive. The attendant rushed Murphy to Dr. J. A. Ellison in Grapevine, but Murphy was dead on arrival.

Texas Highway Patrol Chief, Captain L. G. Phares, was deeply grieved by the loss of his two officers that day. Now he, too, wanted to play a part in bringing down the suspected Bonnie and Clyde. A $1,000.00 reward was immediately offered, along with a description of the vehicle.

Captain Phares had heard about Lee Simmons hiring the highly respected lawman Frank Hamer as a special investigator for the state to develop a plan to stop Bonnie and Clyde's bloody rampages. He immediately called Hamer and begged to be part of the group of lawmen Hamer was forming.

"Frank, you have to let me assign one of my men to join you. Those bastards killed two of my young officers in cold blood!"

Although Hamer did not like being pushed to accept one of Captain Phares' men, he knew that some of them had formerly served as Texas rangers, as he did, so he decided he just might need some level-headed assistance.

Texas Highway Patrolman Manny Gault was selected to serve, and immediately began giving Hamer suggestions as to how best track and locate Bonnie and Clyde. Simmons recognized early on that Hamer and Gault were going to need additional help tracking and capturing these wily criminals. The men were not familiar enough with them to recognize Bonnie and Clyde, or any of their outlaw associates. Simmons contacted the Dallas courts for suggestions. Judge Williams called in Sheriff Smoot Schmit and asked him to find two lawmen to recommend to Hamer. Deputy Bob Alcorn, who knew Bonnie and Clyde on sight, along with Deputy Ted Hinton, who knew the Barrow family, were selected. Both Alcorn and Hinton had been involved with chasing Bonnie and Clyde for over two years, and were elated to be chosen to serve with such an elite group of lawmen, all working toward the capture of this elusive couple.

The four men—Hamer, Simmons, Alcorn, and Hinton—met secretly to discuss ideas on how to best approach the capture or the "bring down" of Bonnie and Clyde and the other gang members. During one of their meetings, Simmons and Hamer discussed the possibility of somehow getting one of the less loyal gang members to betray them. Simmons explained to Hamer, "I have the Governor's permission to grant clemency if someone helps us."

Upon hearing this, Henry Methvin's name was the first to pop into Hamer's mind. Methvin's family lived in northwestern Louisiana, and Hamer knew that Methvin was a relatively new member of the Barrow Gang and had not yet proven himself, and perhaps hadn't developed any deep loyalties to Bonnie and Clyde.

Hamer contacted an old friend, Henderson Jordan, Sheriff of Bienville Parish, Louisiana, where the Methvins lived. Jordan knew Henry Methvin's father well, so he easily set up a meeting with Hamer and Methvin's dad to discuss his possible help in capturing Bonnie and Clyde in exchange for having some of the many charges against his boy dropped.

The men talked for a long time while sitting on park benches around the Arcadia, Louisiana, courthouse.

"Bonnie and Clyde are sooner or later going to get your boy killed, Mr. Methvin," Hamer quietly told him.

Mr. Methvin, after spitting his tobacco, answered only, "I don't want my boy ever having to go back to prison if I help you."

"We can fix that," Hamer assured the older Methvin. The agreement was made between the two men.

The lawmen began planning how best to pull off the dangerous job of stopping Bonnie and Clyde and their gang in such a way as to not kill or injure innocent bystanders. At the time the agreement between Hamer and Methvin was made and confirmed by Texas Governor Ferguson, neither Lee Simmons nor the Governor knew that it was Henry Methvin who killed the two Dallas highway patrolmen near Grapevine.

The agreement between Methvin and the State of Texas authorities was about much more than prison terms for the younger Methvin. The agreement to betray his friends meant the difference between life and death for him because Henry certainly would have been given a death sentence had he been captured and tried for the killings of the patrolmen.

The four posse men were actively sharing ideas, theories, and known patterns of behavior and movements of Bonnie and Clyde. Since Methvin was still with them, the officers believed the group would be traveling north, bound for their old western Arkansas or eastern Oklahoma hideouts on their way to Methvin's family in northwest Louisiana.

On the morning of April 5, 1934, the fugitives were reported seen in Commerce, Oklahoma. Other citizens reported seeing them in and around Miami, Oklahoma, and later they were reported to be parked and resting on the Old Lost Mine Trail. The group most likely would have gone by unnoticed had they not waved guns at a passing vehicle when they attempted to stop it. It had been raining a great deal, and their car had slid off the road into a mud bank. Clyde and Methvin could not free the car, so they were just going to steal another one. The folks in the passing car reported the incident to Miami, Oklahoma, Police Chief Percy Boyd, and he and Constable Cal Campbell drove out to investigate.

The car was still stuck in the mud when Chief Boyd and Constable Campbell arrived. They got out of their car and, with guns drawn, began walking slowly to the Barrow vehicle. Henry and Clyde both opened car doors to use as shields and began firing at the two lawmen, first with shotguns and then with their automatic rifles.

Constable Campbell was the first to die. Soon after, a local trucker, Charles Dobson, stopped to offer assistance. Henry walked around the car and helped the badly wounded Chief Boyd to his feet. While the trucker was instructing Methvin on how to use the chain he had to pull the car out of the mud, another car driven by Jack Boydston drove alongside. Clyde pointed his Browning rifle at the man while telling him to get out of his car. Since it was obvious that Clyde and Henry were desperate and that he could expect no help from the badly wounded lawman, Boydston did what was no doubt the wisest thing by turning over his automobile to Clyde. Clyde ordered Chief Boyd to get into the Boydston vehicle. Blood was noticeably flowing down the left side of Boyd's face and onto his chest as he stumbled over to the Boydston car and climbed in.

Clyde yelled for Bonnie to grab what she could and get into the new car quickly. After Clyde and Methvin had gathered the arsenal of weapons from their stuck car, the four sped away toward Miami, Oklahoma, leaving the trucker Charles Dobson and Jack Boydston standing astonished along the roadside, with the bloody corpse of Cal Campbell lying nearby.

Chief Boyd, the Barrow's unwilling passenger, reported that he was amazed at Clyde Barrow's coolness under such pressure. He also reported that he did not like Clyde's arrogance. "He acted like he owned the world," Boyd stated. It is probably safe to assume this arrogance was one of Clyde Barrow's main personality traits, a trait that no doubt kept him alive for so long, even though he was continually confronted with what would be insurmountable odds if faced by anyone whose arrogance didn't meet the level of Clyde's.

Chief Boyd also reported that he asked Bonnie if she had anything to tell the newspapers if they got away.

"You damn right. Tell the paper I don't smoke cigars. The Joplin papers spread that rumor after finding the pictures we left in Joplin. I just took the cigar from Clyde for the picture."

Clyde managed their escape over into Kansas, and even though they were sighted in several locations, they found their way to Bartlett, where they stopped briefly for food and gasoline before heading toward Fort Scott. Dozens of lawmen were soon covering highways throughout Kansas, Oklahoma, and Arkansas.

Rumors of the many sightings and the number of lawmen being required for the manhunt to stop the gang soon came to the attention of United States Attorney General Homer Cummings, who called for all investigators and field officers to cooperate with local authorities.

On Friday, April 6, 1934, Clyde stopped the car about nine miles south of Fort Scott, Kansas, and as he turned to look at their hostage Percy Boyd, he said, "You can get out here, Chief. I don't care what you tell the law as long as it is the truth." Boyd nodded and happily exited the vehicle.

After sleeping in their car near Fort Scott, Clyde, Bonnie, and Methvin headed toward Stillwell, Oklahoma, where they selected different areas in the Cookson Hills to rest and relax for several days.

The pursuit of Bonnie and Clyde grew more and more intense after the killing of the two Texas patrolmen and the death of Constable Campbell. Citizens throughout Kansas, Oklahoma, Texas, and Arkansas were demanding that lawmen somehow put a stop to these crafty outlaws. Although

Hamer and his small, dedicated force were drawing closer to their prey, the whole country was beginning to think our law enforcement agencies simply could not control such rampant crime.

Clyde Barrow, leader of the Barrow Gang. (Photo courtesy of Dallas Public Library)

⊰18⊱

THE LAST JOURNEY HOME

Bonnie's constant demands that Clyde take her to visit her mother just one more time probably caused Clyde to make their dangerous last journey to Texas after stealing a car in Kansas. As they drove by the Barrow station, they threw out a bottle with a note inside, as was their custom. The note outlined a safe location and time for the last family gathering there would be before the deaths of Bonnie and Clyde.

Word of the gathering was passed among Parker and Barrow relatives by telephone. Almost all of their relatives came to see their loved ones for what they must have felt would be the last time. Bonnie, too, must have sensed that their end was near as she gave her mother a special poem at the meeting of the families. As the evening sun set in the west, Clyde told everyone that they had to leave. As Clyde pulled away with Bonnie and Henry, Bonnie yelled out, "We will be back in two weeks, I promise." That promise was never fulfilled, and the families never saw Bonnie and Clyde alive again.

⚜19⚜

THE STAGE IS SET

Henry Methvin loved his father, Ivan, and had always hoped to help the man find a better lot in life. Few neighbors knew Ivan Methvin, or anything much about him, other than he was a logger, owned an old logging truck, had a son in a Texas prison, and stayed drunk most of the time. But the solitary old man certainly loved his boy Henry, and possibly felt tremendous guilt for not being a better father to him.

When Henry Methvin was a teenager, he was a member of the Barnett Springs Baptist Church in Ruston, Louisiana. He was well liked in school until the hard times of the depression era seemingly changed him, as it did many youths of that period. Seeking a way to improve his situation, Henry became a hobo, traveling west on rail cars and sleeping in hobo camps around the country. While traveling with other hobos, young Methvin attempted his first robbery in order to get food. He was caught and sent to jail, which is where he first met Clyde Barrow, who shared Henry's despondence. Their acquaintance was only a casual one until after Methvin joined Clyde in the jail break to follow.

Bonnie and Clyde had used up most of their former hiding places and friends who might have once offered them a safe retreat. Henry wanted to see his old man again, and convinced Clyde to travel to Louisiana to hide out in the small Methvin cabin for a few days.

Ivan Methvin fully expected his son to be killed if he continued his association with Bonnie and Clyde. He also believed that the only way out for his son was to cooperate with lawmen in a carefully contrived plan to put a stop to the couple's killing spree.

A trap was set for Bonnie and Clyde on May 23, 1934. The posse appointed to bring a conclusion to this tragic story was to be led by Frank Hamer, the highly respected former Texas Ranger. Other posse members chosen by Hamer were Texas lawmen Bob Alcorn and Ted Hinton; Bienville Parish, Louisiana, lawmen Prentice M. Oakley and Henderson Jordan, along with lawman Manny Gault.

The scheme to bring the couple's gangster escapades to a conclusion had been planned by the posse for many months, and the day before their planned attack, lawmen quietly checked into an Arcadia hotel to wait for final directions. Sometime during the night, the men drove to a location along the Jamestown-Sailes Highway, about eight miles from Gibsland. There the men carefully set up behind an earthen embankment at the top of a small hill that was overgrown with brush and trees. They anxiously waited to carry out their assignment—to bring down Bonnie and Clyde forever.

Ivan Methvin had warned his son to not bring Bonnie and Clyde back home with him when they went into Arcadia on the morning of May 23, 1934. Henry may not have known his father's exact plan, or the extent of his father's involvement, but he did know he must somehow disappear if he was to live.

⌘20⌘

AND SO IT WAS FINISHED

At a specific location on a small hill along the east side of the highway a few miles south of Gibsland, on the fateful morning of May 23, 1934, six posse men were to hide behind an earthen, brush-covered bank and wait for their ambush to unfold. Henry's father, Ivan Methvin, had secretly met with posse men Frank Hamer and Ted Hinton on several occasions around the region to discuss ambush plans.

Frank Hamer was armed with a Browning Automatic Rifle and a Remington Model 11 automatic shotgun. Posse man Manny Gault carried a Remington Model 8 Police Special 35-20 shot caliber. Lawman Bob Alcorn carried a Remington Model 8. Ted Hinton had one of the Browning Automatic Rifles loaned to the posse by the Texas National Guard. Henderson Jordan used a Winchester Model 94 30.30 carbine. Prentice Oakley carried a Remington Model 8 with a five-round clip.

The men gathered at the location before midnight the day before, and, after carefully hiding their cars in the woods surrounding the ambush site, they were carefully directed to their places. They cut brush for a blind and crouched down behind it to await the sunrise of May 23, 1934. Soon after Bonnie, Clyde, and Henry left for Gibsland,

Henry's father Ivan drove his old truck to the ambush location, jacked up a tire, and pretended to be fixing a flat.

Bonnie, Clyde, and Henry Methvin left their hideout for Gibsland. In town, Bonnie and Clyde entered a sandwich shop, but decided to bag the sandwiches and leave when Clyde spotted a police car on the street. Clyde's sixth sense told him it was time to depart. Henry Methvin had made good his escape from the pair simply by not returning to the sandwich shop to join them. Shortly after 8:30 A.M., Clyde headed south, down Sailes Road, toward the Methvin farm.

The officers were growing restless. They had been at the blind for nine hours. As the sun rose higher in the sky, the heat was becoming unbearable. They decided to wait a short while longer, then abandon the ambush.

Around 9:00 A.M., a car was heard approaching, traveling at a high rate of speed. The lookout, an officer stationed down the road, studied the passing automobile and identified the driver as Clyde Barrow. He signaled to the hidden officers, and they readied their weapons.

Clyde recognized Ivan Methvin's log truck and slowed to see if the old man needed help. Both Bonnie and Clyde's attentions were focused on Methvin, a diversion that allowed the officers to stand to their feet. Methvin dove under his truck for cover, and Clyde Barrow turned to face the movement on the opposite side of the road. In unison, six officers began to fire into the car. The automobile rocked at the combined impact, as dozens of high-velocity rounds punched through and found their mark. Clyde was hit repeatedly through the head, neck, and torso, and must have died instantly.

Bonnie also received multiple bullet wounds to her head, including a wound to the mouth, which split her mouth to the jaw and embedded her teeth in the opposite door. Another bullet exited through the top of her head. It was reported that as the bullets pierced her flesh, Bonnie emitted a long, haunting scream. So tenaciously had the pair clung to the light of life, she would not submit gently to the darkness of death.

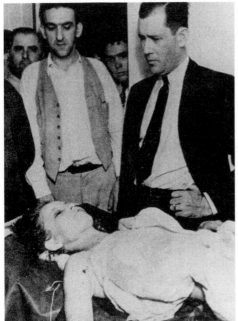

The body of Bonnie Parker in a morgue soon after she was killed by a lawman ambush on May 23, 1934. (Photo courtesy of Dallas Public Library)

Bonnie and Clyde's riddled death car near Gibsland, Louisiana. (Photo courtesy of Dallas Public Library)

The metal jacketed bullets from the officers' Browning Automatic Rifles cut plugs of metal out of the car, and the two bodies were riddled with the shrapnel. Each body was pierced over 40 times by bullets and shrapnel. Many of the bullets had passed through the both of them. Clyde's head hung lifeless out the window. Bonnie was missing a finger, and one of her hands was nearly amputated. Bits of flesh were embedded in the cloth upholstery throughout the interior of the vehicle.

Officers approached and examined the pair for signs of life. Ted Hinton reported that Bonnie was gasping her last breath when he opened the passenger door. Her torso was leaned forward, and her head dangled between her knees. One hand still gripped a sandwich from the Gibsland sandwich shop. A pair of sunglasses, damaged by the gunfire, hung from her face. The bodies were splattered with their own blood, and Clyde Barrow's shirt was dotted with holes.

Guns and other weapons found in Bonnie and Clyde's car after they were killed. (Photo courtesy of Dallas Public Library)

Clyde Barrow was 25 at the time of his death. Bonnie Parker was 23.

Posse men described a deafening silence for several minutes after the firing ceased. No one, it seemed, wanted to be the first to comment or the first to inspect the car and its passengers.

A funeral home in Arcadia made arrangements to pull the riddled Ford V-8 into the city, where hundreds gathered to view the death car and the unrecognizable figures within. Though it seems

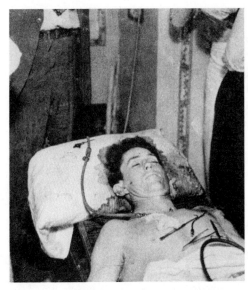

The corpse of Clyde Barrow shortly after he was killed from ambush by a posse near Gibsland, Louisiana. (Photo courtesy of Dallas Public Library)

Dallas Sheriff Smoot Schmidt (second from left) looking over the Bonnie and Clyde death car with other Texas lawmen. (Photo courtesy of Dallas Public Library)

gruesome to us today, several older citizens reported that the car and the remains of Bonnie and Clyde were even viewed by school children when traffic stopped the car near a school playground. Some have furthermore stated that some students fainted, while others vomited or were greatly affected emotionally by the experience.

The families of Bonnie and Clyde were notified in Dallas, and they arranged for the return of their remains with an abundance of support from Texas and Louisiana lawmen. Clyde's remains were delivered to the Sparkman, Holtz and Brand Funeral Home in Dallas before he was interred in the Western Heights Cemetery there. Bonnie's funeral arrangements were handled by the McKamy-Campbell Funeral Home, and her remains were first placed in the Fishtrap Cemetery. Later, in the 1940s, Bonnie's mother, Emma Parker, had Bonnie's remains moved to the Crown Hill Cemetery in Dallas.

Bonnie's sister Billie had had twin daughters who died as children, and were buried with Bonnie in the same grave, although no grave marker exists for the children, or for Bonnie's mother, who was buried next to her daughter.

Marie Barrow Scoma points out the grave of Bonnie Parker to Phillip Steele in the Crown Hill Cemetery in Dallas. (Photo courtesy of Mrs. Phillip Steele)

Bonnie Parker's grave in Crown Hill Cemetery, Dallas, Texas. (Photo courtesy of Phillip Steele)

Hundreds attended the funeral of Bonnie Parker at the Lamar and Smith Funeral Home in Dallas. Bonnie's remains were interred at the Crown Hill Cemetery in Dallas. (Photo courtesy of Dallas Public Library)

Clyde's funeral in Dallas. (Photo courtesy of Dallas Public Library)

Henry Barrow at son Clyde's grave shortly after burial in Western Heights Cemetery in Dallas. (Photo courtesy of Marie Barrow Scoma)

Clyde's mother at his grave shortly after burial in the Western Heights Cemetery in Dallas. (Photo courtesy of Marie Barrow Scoma)

CLYDE BARROW'S DEATH SHIRT

Clyde's "Death Shirt" is on display as a part of the Bonnie & Clyde "Death Car" display at Whiskey Pete's Hotel & Casino in Primm, Nevada (35 minutes south of Las Vegas). (Photo courtesy of Primadonna Resorts)

Author Phillip Steele at Clyde and Buck Barrow's graves in Western Heights Cemetery in Dallas. (Photo courtesy of Mrs. Phillip Steele)

Marie Barrow Scoma at Western Heights Cemetery where her parents and brothers are buried in Dallas. (Photo courtesy of Phillip Steele)

Bonnie and Clyde ambush posse. Left to right, standing: Prentis Oakley, Ted Hinton, Bob Alcorn, and Manny Gault. Left to right, kneeling: Frank Hamer and Henderson Jordon. (Photo courtesy of Dallas Public Library)

Some of the posse that ambushed Bonnie and Clyde, looking over license plates, magazines, and other items found in the death car. Left to right: Sheriff Smoot Smith with Deputies Ed Caster, Ted Hinton, and Bob Alcorn. (Photo courtesy of Dallas Public Library)

⇥21⇤

WHATEVER HAPPENED
TO HENRY?

Many feel that the worst thing Henry Methvin ever did in his life was to betray his friends Bonnie and Clyde by helping to arrange their downfall. After the ambush, Methvin's crimes in Texas were pardoned, as promised by the Governor to Henry's father. Oklahoma, though, was not involved in the bargaining for the capture of Bonnie and Clyde. Henry was tried in Oklahoma and sentenced to die for his crimes there, but his mother was able to plead her son's sentence down to ten years.

After his release and brief attempt at managing a restaurant, the always nervous and despondent Methvin again chose the life of a hobo and became an alcoholic addicted to cheap wine—perhaps to escape his past memories. Soon after he rejoined the hobo community, Methvin's badly chopped up body was found scattered up the railroad tracks near Lake Charles, Louisiana. Many believe his death to have been a deliberate one at the hands of some of his hobo friends who felt he had it coming for betraying Bonnie and Clyde.

Bonnie and Clyde. (Photo courtesy of the Texas-Dallas History Archives)

EPILOGUE

Certainly Bonnie Parker and Clyde Barrow were hardened, and sometimes heartless, criminals who caused great suffering and hardship far beyond that of the economic depression our nation was struggling with at that time. Records indicate that, although most of their murders were committed in some sort of self-defense "setting," Bonnie and Clyde killed innocent people on many occasions. Why then did Bonnie and Clyde have such wide literary appeal and create such a nationwide curiosity that remains strong, even today?

Perhaps the answer lies in the fact that Bonnie and Clyde were ill-fated young lovers who, for whatever reasons, were driven to crime by the terrible jobless conditions brought about by the Great Depression. Of course, this reasoning cannot be justified or tolerated by society's laws that are enforced for the good of the masses. Thousands of other Americans in similar circumstances found a way to survive without turning to crime.

Perhaps, then, it is because society in general does not like a coward, a traitor, or a back-stabber, and perhaps the American people would have better supported the ambush tactics of the law enforcement authorities if their plans for

145

capturing or bringing down Bonnie and Clyde had been more open and forthright. The fact that their friend Henry Methvin helped trap the couple, and that Methvin's father set up the ambush, was not looked upon by the general public as an upright way to bring down the criminals. Similar stories of "traitor" friends can be found in the accounts of Jesse James, "Pretty Boy" Floyd, John Wesley Hardin, Belle Starr, "Wild Bill" Hickock, John Dillinger, Abraham Lincoln, and other personalities who have become icons in our nation's history.

Because the story of Bonnie and Clyde has been so romanticized by the multitude of fictional accounts of their lives, it is difficult to lay down a factual account, such as Marie and I hope we have done here, and, at the same time, somehow capture the magic of fictional romance in truthful reporting. At any rate, it is first this author's desire that Marie Barrow Scoma, my coauthor, who unfortunately passed away before seeing the entire text, would be pleased. Secondly, it is my hope that the general readership will not only now have a better understanding of these historical personalities, but will also be entertained for a period of time.

PHILLIP W. STEELE
WITH
MARIE BARROW SCOMA

Coauthors of this text, Marie Barrow Scoma with Phillip W. Steele. (Photo courtesy of Mrs. Phillip Steele, January 1999, Mesquite, Texas)

BIBLIOGRAPHY

BOOKS

Bain, George F. *The Barrow Gang: The Real Story,* 1968.

Draper, W. R. and Mabel. *The Blood Soaked Career of Bonnie Parker,* Haldeman-Julius Publications, Girard, Kansas, 1946.

Fortune, Jan I. and Nelson Algren. *The True Story of Bonnie and Clyde,* The New American Library, 1968.

Frost, Gordon and John H. Jenkins. *I'm Frank Hamer,* State House Press, Austin, Texas, 1993.

Hinton, Ted. *Ambush: The Real Story of Bonnie and Clyde,* Shoal Creek Press, Bryant, Texas.

Hounschell, Jim. *Lawmen and Outlaws: 116 Years of Joplin History,* Joplin, Missouri Police Force.

Louderback, Lew. *The Bad Ones,* Fawcett Publications, Inc., Greenwich, Conn.

Milner, E. R. *The Lives and Times of Bonnie and Clyde,* Southern Illinois University Press, 1996.

Nash, Jay Robert. *Bloodletters and Badmen,* M. Evans and Co., N.Y., Publishers.

Parkers, Mrs. Emma, L. J. Cowen, and Nell Barrow Cowen. *Fugitives: The Story of Clyde Barrow and Bonnie Parker,* first printing, September 1934, The Ranger Press, Publishers.

Phillips, John Neal. *Running with Bonnie and Clyde: The Ten Fast Years of Ralph Fultz,* University of Oklahoma Press, 1949.

Sifakis, Carl. *Encyclopedia of American Crime,* Smithmark Publishers, 1992.

Underwood, Sidney. *Depression Desperados,* Eakin Press, Austin, Texas.

NEWSPAPERS

Commerce News, Commerce, Oklahoma, April 12, 1934.

Daily Oklahoman, Oklahoma City, Oklahoma, June 12, 1938.

Dallas Morning News, Dallas, Texas, May 24, 1934 and May 26, 1996.

Enid Morning News, Enid, Oklahoma, July 27, 1933.

Fort Worth Star Telegram, "Clyde Barrow Speaks Out," Marie Barrow, May 23, 1998.

Indian Citizen Democrat, Atoka, Oklahoma, June 12, 1938.

Northwest Arkansas Times, several issues.

Ruston Daily Leader, Ruston, Louisiana, "The Story of Bonnie and Clyde," Thomas E. Aswell, 1934.

Shreveport Journal, Shreveport, Louisiana, May 23 and 24, 1934, and May 10, 1984.

Tulsa World, Tulsa, Oklahoma, November 19, 1998, John Wooley.

PERIODICALS

Butler, Ken. "Bonnie and Clyde," *Oklahombre's Quarterly.*

Fischer, Bob with Sandy Jones. "It's Death to Bonnie and Clyde," *Oklahombre's Quarterly,* Winter 1999, Volume 2, Number 2.

Mattex, Rick. "Bonnie and Clyde in Oklahoma," *Oklahombre's Quarterly,* Winter 1991.

Neal, Joseph C. *Laws and Outlaws,* Shiloh Museum publication, 1988.

Perrin, Tony. "Barrow Gang in Arkansas," *Oklahombre's Quarterly.*

Playboy Magazine, W. D. Jones Story, November 1968.

INTERVIEWS

Blalock, Warren, Historian, Alma, Arkansas

Brown, Betty

Brown, George, Little Rock, Arkansas

Brown, Robert L., Jr., Mineral Wells, Texas

Cooper, Ann Brown, Fayetteville, Arkansas

Davis, Johnathan, Dallas, Texas

Dowis, Weldon, Hot Springs, Arkansas, age 95 in 1999, former commander Texas National Guard Unit

Heard, Charles, Dallas, Texas

Joyner, Lorraine, Gibsland, Louisiana

Montgomery, Wanda Audit, California

Perrin, Tony, Arkansas

Scoma, Marie Barrow, age 81 in 1999, Mesquite, Texas

Scoma, Shawn, Mesquite, Texas

Stewart, Flo, Longview, Texas

Williams, Buddy, Mesquite, Texas

LETTERS

Family letters owned by Marie Barrow Scoma

Chapler, Keith M., M.D., Chapler-Osborn Clinic, Dexter, Iowa, May 3, 1974

INDEX

Summers, U.S.
    Congressman Hatton, 117
Swift, Texas, 21

T

Teleco, Texas, 27
Temple, 88
Temple, Texas, 63
Texas, 43, 63, 81, 130
Texas Federal Prison, 45
Texas Highway Patrol, 124
Texas National Guard, 117
Texas Ranger, 68
Texas State Penitentiary, 33
Texas State Prison, 72
The Brown Cracker and
    Candy Company, 30
*The Story of Bonnie and
    Clyde*, 52
Thomas, Robert, 43
Thornton, Roy, 37
Trammell, Ewell, 98
Turner, 41, 42, 43
Turner, William, 40

U

United Glass, 30
University of Arkansas, 96

V

Van Buren, Arkansas, 103
Van Noy, Texas Ranger, 68

W

Waco, Texas, 31, 38, 39, 42,
    43, 45
Waldo, 85, 86
Walker, Cumie , 21
Walker, Henry, 21
Washington County,
    Arkansas, 96
Wellington, 91
Western Heights Cemetery,
    114, 138
Western Union, 30, 42
Westmoreland Street, 69
Wheeler, E. B., 124
Wichita, Kansas, 105
Wichita Falls, Texas, 42, 56,
    62
Wilson, Weber, 101
Winchester, 101
Winslow, 71, 100
Witherspoon, Sergeant
    Thomas, 107
Worcester, Massachusetts,
    48
Worley, Olin, 122

Y

Yost, Trustee, 118